DOUNDALE!

A Guide for Black Immigrants Navigating
Money and the System in the United States

By Yannick Diouf

Please note that this book is for informational purposes only and should not be used to make personal financial decisions. Readers should consult with a financial professional in order to get advice tailored to their particular circumstances.

Copyright © 2023 Yannick Diouf

All rights reserved.

No part of this book can be transmitted or reproduced in any form including print, electronic, photocopying, scanning, mechanical or recording without prior written permission from the author.

Table of Contents

Foreword 6

Dedication 9

Thank You and Acknowledgments 13

Purpose 15

Background 18

What's Your Relationship $tatus with Money? 23

Start With $5 29

Issa WHOLE Budget 34

Creating Your Safety Nets 58

Getting Out of Debt 89

Getting Into Debt 101

Investing 122

Your Journey: Doing What's Best For You 144

"Nah"... Setting Boundaries For Future You 149

Money Shouldn't Be Taboo 159

Understanding Amerikkka 165

Money and Disabilities 185

Women and Money 197

CONCLUSION 207

The Concept 210

Book Summary 215

References 223

Foreword

It is a singular moment for me as an American citizen, born and raised in the States, to write this foreword and bless this book. I've known Yannick Diouf and his family since he was a boy, and I was taking him and his younger brother Jeremy to grade school. For the past twenty plus years, we've celebrated milestones, witnessed setbacks, and marked with pride the accomplishments that contributed to his growth. He was always determined to pursue the path set before him with excellence. The exuberance that Yannick uses to do almost anything he sets out to achieve is another lesson we can all take from this young author. He steadily proves all the adages such as *"Anything is possible"*, *"If you believe it, you can achieve it,"* etc. Yannick is the epitome of the American Dream, as it is intended to be.

No matter what your background may be, every reader can learn from the author and this book about the power of possibility and the conversion that takes place through focused intention in the work that is inevitably required.

It is such a message of hope in this incredibly challenging new decade in America. Lead the way, Yannick. We are following you. #Aspire.

Saundra L. Lamb, Esq.

Dedication

I was born in Dakar, Senegal, and came to the United States in the year 2000 with my family. Due to the broken immigration system, I became undocumented, and lived with that status for the majority of my time here in the United States. My status influenced and defined much of my experience in this country. My family and I faced many challenges as we struggled to achieve our education and live a stable life.

Our long journey is reminiscent of that of my maternal grandmother, Marie Basseck, who made the long trip from her native village, Boula, in Guinea Bissau, to the capital of Senegal, Dakar, in the 1950s. At the age of 17, she got married and gave birth to a boy, then a girl, before giving birth to triplets (three boys). At that time, having triplets was almost non-existent and considered a source of misfortune.

At 22 years old, Marie Basseck had been tested by a difficult pregnancy and the birth of her triplets, which was an extraordinary event in the community. She now had to meet the needs of her eldest son, her daughter, and her triplets. She became an entrepreneur by selling fish and charcoal. This became quite lucrative for her, which helped to take care of her children. However, she remained convinced that her life, and the future of her children, lay elsewhere.

Because of the difficulties and precariousness of her life, she planned to leave Boula to pass through Casamance, and join her family in Dakar, the capital of Senegal. She managed to save money from her coal business to pay for her trip. While in Dakar, she met her husband, David Ndey (my grandfather), a good and loving man. With his salary as a tailor, and Marie's entrepreneurial spirit, they were able to create a blended family where happiness and peace have always reigned. From there, my mother and her three additional siblings were born.

Over the past two decades that I have lived in the United States, I have witnessed similar levels of conviction from my mother, Germaine Ndey, as she and the family fought to make sure we attained our education. Whilst having to navigate a new system and not speaking English in a brand new country. Regardless of the obstacles, the same vision my grandmother had of herself and her children was what my mother and the family had for us: the dream of a better life.

With support, I was able to graduate from high school, then received my associates from Montgomery College, and my bachelor's degree in business from the University of Maryland, College Park. While in college, I couldn't work or qualify for most scholarships, let alone the FAFSA. Nonetheless, I got involved in the immigrant rights movement and volunteered for the Maryland DREAM Act campaign of 2012, which eventually passed. My senior year of college, a few friends and I decided to organize a conference for undocumented Black immigrants, which we used as the catalyst to create an organization called the UndocuBlack Network, which I helped run for five years. After all the sacrifices and hardships caused by the immigration system, I was the first in my family to graduate.

I have now been working in the housing finance industry for six years, which was made possible by my mother, Germaine. I dedicate this book to her, the family, and my grandmother, especially, whose shoulders we all stand on.

Thank You and Acknowledgments

I would like to acknowledge all of the people who have contributed to this book and helped me in writing it:

My mother, **Germaine Ndey,** for being an inspiration, and to whom this book is dedicated.

Contributing Editors: A huge thanks to **Alvin Fonkoua** and **Byron Jackson** for lending their expertise for the book over the past 2 years. Alvin's financial knowledge and Byron's knowledge on the history of race in the U.S. have proven to be invaluable.

Chief Book Editor: **Jamie Richards-Linton** for her expertise in formatting and editing the book.

Copy Editor: **Yasmin Yonis** for using journalistic skills to make content suggestions and edits.

Marketing: **DeShawna Grimsley** for her marketing expertise and **Jeremy Diouf**, CEO at

Synergy Reach, for his expertise in online marketing and web design.

Book Cover Design: **Sidra Fatima** for using her amazing design skills to create the book cover.

Honorable Mentions:

Benjamin Ndugga-Kabuye

My siblings: Colombe Diouf, Jessica Diouf, Jeremy Diouf

Jonathan Jayes-Green

Fithawit Ghebru

Derrick Arthur

Claire Detrick-Jules

Clémence Ndoye

Sandra Lamb

Madelaine Seydi

Cheryl Nam

Purpose

"Doundale" is a word derived from Wolof, the main language spoken in Senegal, which means to live and thrive. The book outlines how to set up a holistic financial management plan within the socio-economic context experienced by Black immigrants, so they not only survive, but *thrive* by understanding the rules of the game.

"We did not come all the way to the United States to be broke. Get your degree and make that money." As a Black immigrant, this is something we hear all too often. Whether it's right or wrong, the pressure to succeed is a reality that we live in. This book provides guidance for Black immigrants on structuring their personal finances with the context of living in the U.S. Oftentimes, Black immigrants (like other immigrant groups) are not aware that there are rules to the game, or know how the economic system is structured; therefore, time is wasted, money is lost, and mistakes are made. I focus on Black immigrants, specifically, because (wait for it) I am a Black immigrant and I have had a unique experience living in the U.S. that is very

different from that of a non-Black immigrant. In a country, such as the U.S., which is built on racism, it is important to name and be very specific about what Black immigrants experience. Creating a resource for "everyone" instead of specifically for Black people is ineffective, and doesn't take into consideration our lived experiences that affect our financial circumstances. "Everyone" is code for whiteness, since white people are the dominant default group in the U.S. This is because racism discounts Black lives, and therefore, Black experiences. Think of racism like a river of resources going from A to C; if water is not intentionally diverted to B, then Black people don't get any of that water/resources.

For the purposes of this book, I will be referring to Black immigrants as anyone of African descent, who has immigrated to the U.S. as first or second generation. It is common for some Black immigrants to not identify themselves as "Black," but rather, as their respective nationality. Nonetheless, the U.S. does not differentiate between types of Black people, because Black is Black. U.S. institutions have firmly placed Black immigrants in the same oppressed and marginalized grouping as African Americans, and others that look and identify as Black. So, regardless of if you consider yourself Ethiopian, Jamaican, Senegalese, or South African, it will make very little difference in how you are perceived in the U.S.

In this book, I discuss the basics of financial management, making financial decisions, and navigating the system in the U.S. to ultimately increase your chances of success, and have less financial stress in your life. I believe in the power of having a robust financial plan, making prudent financial decisions, and having solid investments, as your finances touch almost *every* aspect of your life. Your finances, therefore, also have a big impact on your quality of life, including your mental health.

Background

A big part of me writing this book is rooted in a desire to share the relief that having a financial management system has brought me. Stress can and does manifest into physical symptoms that cause illness and suffering. Having a plan has drastically reduced my anxiety around money, and I believe it can do the same for you. Granted, this is only a part of the equation to being less stressed (along with exercise, eating well, etc.), it is nonetheless, a huge part of it.

If you feel that your finances run you instead of the other way around, you are not alone. There is a culture of dysfunction when it comes to financial management in the U.S., in large part because financial literacy and education is not widespread, which leads to the mismanagement of funds and bad decisions being made. This, combined with the historical precedence of Black institutions being systemically stymied, has created an environment where there is a lack of trust of financial institutions, in addition to a lack of educational resources from these institutions. Take for example the collapse of the Freedman's Bank—the first national bank for emancipated Black people: white corruption in the bank led to Black people's savings and deposits being used to fund loans for white people, but not Black people. The bank issued unsecured loans to large industries that defaulted, which led to Black depositors losing an estimated total of $22 million in savings by modern calculations. Many Black depositors lost life savings and were not reimbursed by the bank or the federal government. The failure of the bank in the 1870s impacted Black U.S. citizens' trust in financial institutions, which continues until this day.

While having a good financial plan is important and can improve your life, it is important to acknowledge that wages in the U.S have stagnated since the 1980s, and people are not being paid adequately as a result of many factors. So, regardless of how much financial planning that you do, if your wages are not enough to support your basic living expenses, it will always be a losing game. And, part of that is out of our control. With that said, these macro issues should not stop you from achieving your financial goals. They will definitely hinder you, but shouldn't stop you.

While the average person in the U.S. may struggle to manage their finances, it can be especially difficult among Black immigrants as we are less likely to have the experience, the lessons, and the funds passed down to us from generation to generation to help us navigate the system. This book aims to solve only a part of that by providing the basic foundation of financial management and knowledge on how the system works and why. You will not find all of the answers to your financial questions in this book, nor is it intended to provide all of the answers. Instead, this book highlights the beginning steps of creating your financial plans. The reason I say this book only addresses a part of financial management is because it is a topic that can be cut in a thousand directions. I can write a whole entire book specifically on investing, debt, or budgeting. However, it is more efficient for me to briefly cover those topics and leave it to your discretion to decide what to research, focus on, and implement. I've learned that when it comes to finances (and life in general), there are no "right" or "wrong" answers, rather, every decision has its advantages and disadvantages. So, I will focus on big picture items and speak in general terms, based on what is the societal norm, rather than what is specific to each individual. Which is why most things that I mention may have exceptions to them. *Only you can make the best decisions about your finances based on your unique scenario*, so use this book as a tool to help you in that decision-making, and not the sole basis of it. It is not meant to give any specific investment advice that is specific to you. Furthermore, major financial decisions require looking at and analyzing your entire financial picture and lifestyle to make sure whatever you decide is right for you.

I started this chapter by saying there is a culture of dysfunction when it comes to finances, and I will end by saying this dysfunction permeates most aspects of our financial lives (credit cards, student loans, financing purchases, bad decisions, etc.), and is enabled by the lack of proper education from schools, dubious fine print in financial documents, and frivolous, rather than strategic spending. Objectively speaking, credit cards and student loans aren't bad; however, our practices around these huge financial commitments are toxic because many don't have the tools, nor the emotional capacity to manage them effectively, so they get *played*. The good news is that this can be fixed with a few simple changes, but they will be challenging

What's Your Relationship $tatus with Money?

Surviving is a different skill set than thriving.
– Megan DeMatteo

Your relationship with money has a lot to do with *how you grew up with money*. Because we need(ed) money for suya, enjera, jollof, shelter, and most activities, it is likely that your lifestyle as a child or teen, up until now, has been impacted by your access to capital. If you struggled or didn't struggle with money in the past, it will have a direct impact on how you emotionally respond to money. Are you a spender or a saver? Some people grew up poor and are extreme spenders because they are unsure when they will have money again. Others who grow up poor can *also* be extreme savers because of the sense that there is scarcity. And then there is everything in between. "So, your generation, your parents' income, values held, part of the world, state of the economy, power, and circumstance are all factors that can impact how you view and interact with money."[1] The most important thing is to know what your relationship status with money is, because having that insight will allow you to customize your approach to financial management.

What do I mean by this? Let me explain. Personally, during most of my time in the U.S., I have been without much money (thank you immigration system), and that has resulted in me having an incredible sense of paranoia and anxiety around losing money because I know what it's like to be without it. Therefore, I make sure to have a large enough safety net in case I lose my job; I have insurance, and I create multiple financial buffers around me which includes a disciplined approach to spending. Knowing I have this anxiety around money as a direct result of how I grew up helps me know what I need in order to mitigate that anxiety. Every time I think about making a big purchase, I ask myself: Do I really need this? How much will I use it? Can and should it wait? This discipline is a *day to day practice*. These practices are driven by a fear of going back to those days

---

[1]

where I struggled financially. Those days formed my personal relationship with money.

Oftentimes, poor people of color establish their relationship status with money during extreme times in their lives. Death of a loved one may not only be caused by poverty, but also put many people deeper into poverty, as funeral expenses can reach $10,000. Illness and the medical bills that come with that can leave a long-lasting impression and a sense of stress. Experiencing eviction with the shame and stress that comes with that is another event that leaves a long-lasting imprint on one's relationship with money. So, based on your relationship with money, you need to figure out how this impacts your day-to-day, which is, in my opinion, the first step in having an *effective* financial management plan. Know your relationship status with your finances: Are y'all friends or are y'all married? Do you even know of each other's existence?

Take someone who every time they earn $1, they spend $3 and go into debt. I would tell this person, first of all: Do not shame yourself. Sometimes people use spending as a form of therapy, and this should be taken into consideration. Instead, reflect on why you spend the way that you do. What emotions come up for you? Perhaps you should have a limit on shopping in your budget and not go to the extremes of completely cutting shopping off. Or, take someone who is extremely frugal and doesn't spend enough money to take care of their basic needs, to them I would say: Ask yourself why, and how has your relationship with money impacted this? Reflect deeply on why you do not feel worthy of purchasing your basic needs, even though you have the money for it. Or, take someone who does spend enough money, doesn't over-shop, but instead, their priorities are messed up. Meaning, they have credit card debt, they are behind on rent, they don't have a couch, but they spend money on the latest iPhone or PlayStation. In this situation, I would say to this person: This mismatch in priorities may be impacted by your relationship with money, considering that you overspend on luxury items while your basic necessities are not even met. Use this information as you build out your financial plan. I would recommend that you list out the needs in a budget, and rank them as most to least important to make sure the basics are met.

What's Your Relationship $tatus with Money?

CHECK THIS OUT!

Money Trees

"I've learned from talking to hundreds[2] *of people about their money that personal finance is very nuanced. Some people have high debt tolerance, others are more geared toward long-term savings. Some people love a good bargain, while others are motivated by luxury."* - *Megan DeMatteo*

Megan DeMatteo is a money writer and editor at Select, and former freelancer at Business Insider, covering personal finance. DeMatteo writes, "Years later, I realize that many of my mistakes would have been preventable if someone had taught me how to align my money with my goals. Too often, our introduction to personal finance is a set of dogmatic guidelines with little room to personalize your decisions around what actually makes you happy. Families focused on survival know this well, because surviving is a different skill set than thriving. Save 25%

---

[2]

> of your paycheck. Don't buy things you don't need. Don't go on vacations. Only eat food you buy on sale. Wear clothes until they have holes, then learn to sew and mend the holes. Wait for the other shoe to drop, because it always does."
>
> In her description above, it's clear how her family's relationship with money and how she grew up influences her beliefs and behavior with money. As you can see, DeMatteo had to shift how she interacted with money because it was very much influenced by how she grew up. Had she not recognized and changed her dynamic with money, it would have slowed down her growth in managing her finances.

Key Takeaways:

- Your relationship with money is heavily influenced by how you grew up
- Keep this relationship in mind as you build your financial plan
- Use your emotional cues as indicators for what works and what doesn't

Start With $5

Having good overall financial management also requires a dedication to internal and external self-discovery

The concept of *starting with $5* is a metaphor that represents starting something new in a way that is easily doable. Because so much of money and building new habits is psychological, starting with some tangible easy wins releases dopamine and allows you to move on to the next step with more confidence. This, over time, creates momentum, and ultimately creates conditions for long-term success. Simply put, this means if you are training for a 26 mile marathon by starting out with running 1 mile and increasing your mileage overtime, this will give you momentum and a much greater chance at success, as opposed to starting out by running 10 miles on day one.

Let's take the example of budgeting; by simply knowing a ballpark amount of your income and expenses can be a huge step in the right direction. When it comes to investing, putting in $5 the first time, while you learn more about investments, can be a good place to start, as opposed to waiting on learning everything before starting to invest. During this learning phase, you should consider brokerages that charge $0 fees. A huge part of managing finances is psychological, and investing hundreds or thousands of dollars can seem like an insurmountable task, which is why starting small represents a "win." Building in small wins gives you momentum to be able to move on to the next step. Small wins add up over time and lead to success, but they don't happen overnight. Megan DeMatteo has interviewed hundreds of experts, including millionaires, and shared,

> "Through this, I've learned that the people who are most successful with money stick to routine habits that operate independently from their emotional highs and lows. No matter what's going on in their life, they contribute to their retirement fund. They make on-time payments. They calculate the interest rate on their mortgage and tighten up their credit score before applying for any kind of loan."

In other words, they do the boring stuff even when it's not so thrilling.

Having good overall financial management also requires a dedication to internal and external self-discovery. In order to figure out what works for you, testing new tools and techniques is part of the external process, and listening to your emotions is an important part of the internal process. Oftentimes, I find that people get discouraged when they try a new financial management system, and they become overwhelmed by it, only to revert to their old ways. This issue can be mitigated by starting at the easiest point. Many people have the unrealistic expectation that they need to get it right the first time, or else they have failed. The truth is that when it comes to managing finances, frustration, setbacks, and failure are necessary parts of the process to get you to a place that works for you, and that will eventually help you to achieve your goals. Think of these frustrations and failures as feedback to yourself that something isn't quite working and that you should make a change. This mindset shift can help you endure the long journey of getting to a good financial place.

Here are some tips that may help you on that journey:

1. Recognize that your starting point doesn't need to be perfect the first time, but as long as you are consistent in your approach and attitude, it can have long-lasting effects.

2. Whether you are trying to invest in stocks or trying to start a budget, start with $5 or start with 15 minutes.

3. Learn and improve as you go along. *Expect* and *embrace* your mistakes. Once these mistakes happen, learn from them, adjust, implement, and move on.

4. This journey in discovery looks different for everyone, and what works for one person could be disastrous for the other. Swim in your own lane, but also learn from others and apply what strategies are in line with your values. Ultimately, different solutions are all valid.

Think of managing finances like going to the gym. You may start with lighter weights, and as you work out, each tear in the muscle rebuilds and grows over time. You may not see results in the first week, or even the first month, but if you are consistent with the small steps, the small wins add up to give you momentum to be in a place that is right for *you*.

Key Takeaways:

- Make managing your finances easy and doable.

- Frustration and setbacks are a part of the process, embrace them!

- Create a breakdown of your financial plan and use small wins as momentum

Issa WHOLE Budget

A budget is a plan of how you will spend your money. It's that simple. I cannot overstate the importance of having a budget - it is simply one of the best ways to manage your money on a day-to-day or week-to-week basis to ultimately help you achieve your long-term goals. A budget allows you to allocate your income to your expenses and long-term goals. It is also a reflection of your values, i.e., what and how much you spend your money on reflects what you care about or value the most. For example, some people decide to cook instead of eating out because it saves them money, which they can then use for lavish trips all over the world. While others blow their money at the club and at restaurants, because they like to have a good time every weekend and could care less about traveling. Neither of these lifestyles is right or wrong, they are merely a reflection of where each person's values lie.

There are two very, very important things to remember about budgeting: First, create a budget that works best for you, and second, start *simple*. It is likely that in the past, you may have tried to make a budget and became frustrated with the process. You may have then forgotten about it, or decided to no longer use it. Remember that failure and setbacks are not only a part of the process, but are absolutely crucial in ultimately helping you create a budget that works for you. Pay attention to your emotions and allow them to guide you to a solution, rather than letting them run you into giving up.

When the budgeting process is clunky and you get frustrated, that's your body telling you that whatever you are doing, something about it isn't working. That is *golden* feedback. You know yourself better than most, so ask yourself: What about this is frustrating? Is it the budget platform? Is it the calculations? Is it the font? Oftentimes, people will take the budget or template from someone else and try to fit their budget in there. There is nothing wrong with starting out with a template that's not yours, but it can be challenging if you're using a template that is not reflective of your lifestyle, financial management plan, or the way your brain works. Depending on who *you* are, your lifestyle, your relationship with money, when and how you get paid, etc., all of these factors may impact what a successful budget looks like for you.

My advice: Start simple. There are so many templates, financial engines, opinions, books (this one included), that it can feel overwhelming. So start *simple*.

The way income is received may influence how you decide to create your budget. Most people are paid biweekly, and so, they create budgets that are tracked by the month. Others, such as students, the unemployed, or people with disabilities, may have a lump sum of money they receive periodically and need to manage it over long periods of time. This, too, can influence how they create their budget. These subtle differences are important to note and be aware of, because ultimately, you need to create something that works for you and this is likely to evolve over time as your needs and lifestyle changes.

Getting Started On Your Budget
Step 1: Be patient

You won't get your budget right the first time, or the second, and maybe not even the third—and that's okay. After the 100th time, you need more than this book, just call me directly. LOL.

Managing your finances, especially if you have not done it before, is a journey that can be compared to a baby learning to walk. I don't expect a 9 month old baby to run like Usain Bolt. Rather, I expect the baby with their cute little Pillsbury arm rolls and Michelin Man legs to stumble and fall many times as they get used to their body. As time passes, that baby will eventually get stronger, start to walk, then run (to ask you for money). So, be kind to yourself, and allow room for learning and stumbling. This doesn't mean keep making the same mistake over and over; rather, it means that if you made a mistake twice, figure out what about the process is leading you to make such a mistake. Treat yourself with patience while also holding yourself accountable. Early on, I realized I was having trouble managing all of my expenses in one account, so I separated my fixed expenses (expenses that stay the same each month) into one bank, and my variable expenses (expenses that vary every month) into another bank account. That way, I put in the amount I need to cover my fixed expenses, and only have to worry about the 8 variable expenses in my other bank account, as opposed to monitoring the total 18 expenses every month.

> ## CHECK THIS OUT!
>
> ### It's Fixed or Variable
>
> Quick Tip: Open two separate bank accounts in which one will have the funds for your fixed expenses, and the other one will have funds for your variable expenses.
>
> Fixed expenses are recurring expenses for which the amount doesn't change month after month. You know exactly what you will pay for your phone, your car insurance, your Wi-Fi, etc. As a result, you can calculate exactly how much your bank account with fixed expenses needs to have each month to cover these bills. Once you calculate this number, you can take it a step further and set up automatic payments to be

> drawn from that account—that way, you don't even have to worry about it.
>
> Variable expenses are recurring expenses that may change slightly every month. You may have similar costs month after month, but there is a shift with some of these costs. This may include gas, groceries, clothes, eating out, etc.
>
> Having these two accounts separated helps to reduce the stress of having to manage so many expenses in one bank account. Now, you only need to really deal with one bank account that houses your variable expenses, while monitoring your fixed automated account. Doing this can reduce a lot of stress, and free up your capacity to focus on other aspects of managing your money.

Step 2: Create your budget

Take an empty excel spreadsheet, or a notebook, or your phone and create large buckets of expense categories that will go into your budget (i.e. rent, food, auto, electricity). These big buckets allow you to organize your expenses in general terms, so you have an idea of how much you are spending in each category. I will warn you, that most times, people severely underestimate how much they spend on each category, especially on food/eating out! This doesn't need to be exact. You just need an educated guess as to where you spend your money each month. Over time, as you continue working on your budget, the numbers will become more and more accurate.

> # CHECK THIS OUT!
>
> ### Your Goals Belong in Your Budget
>
> Quick Tip: You can also include your long-term goals as expense lines. For example, you can allocate a certain amount of money towards a goal, such as saving for a down payment, vacation, or even car repairs. Simply take the total amount for the goal you would like to save, and allocate a certain amount of that in your budget to save every month. By doing this, you are telling your money what to do, as opposed to your money telling *you* what to do.

Step 3: Track your expenses

Track one month's worth of your expenses and tally up the actual amount that was spent. This can be done by looking at your expenses in your bank statements or payment apps (such as PayPal, Venmo, CashApp). If you use mostly cash, or cannot find a trace of your expenses, you may guess as best you can. Then, match the actual expense amounts based on the bucket categories you previously created to get an idea of where your money goes. Remember, you are not looking to be 100% accurate on your first budget, you are trying to get as close as possible. The most important thing is to have a close estimation of what you are spending for the first go around. You can create and implement better tracking systems for future budgets. You most likely will add new categories to your budget and may be surprised by how much you actually spend on certain categories, such as food. All of that is okay.

Now that you have an idea of what budget categories are common and how much you spend each month, you can now start to plan and be strategic for future budgets. As mentioned, the point is not to be perfect the first time. As each month passes, you will become more and more accurate as you track your expenses and learn where your money goes so you can plan/budget for the following month. Always remember to look back at your previous months' expenses to have a sense of how much to budget for in the future.

Tracking your expenses tells the story of where your money is going, gives you insight on your values, and what your behaviors are. Month after month, you can add sections to your excel spreadsheet or notebook that help you manage your money. Tracking expenses is the foundation of getting ahead, because numbers don't lie. They bring you back to a reality we have all tried to escape at least once. Oftentimes, we underestimate how much we spend, and this can be challenging for many, so figure out what works for you.

I personally track all my expenses with bank accounts and I do it every 2 weeks, so I don't become overwhelmed toward the end of the month with tracking a month's worth of expenses. Am I perfect? Absolutely not. Sometimes I miss the two week mark and go the whole month without tracking my expenses. I mention this because sometimes you will fall from your plan, and that's okay. The important thing is to keep moving forward, despite any stumbling blocks you encounter, or any deviations from your plan.

Perhaps you are having difficulties because your budget process isn't a good fit for you. There are those who track their expenses on a weekly basis, monthly basis, and some even do it every day. I advise you to do whatever works best for you. Try tracking every Friday, every 2 weeks, or every month. You will find that the easier you make it on yourself, the more likely you are to stick with the process. Because a big part of financial management is psychological, the harder a process is, and the more hurdles involved, the less likely you are to use that process in the long-term. Which is why I stress to make the process as easy for yourself as possible, especially in the beginning.

Once you have your budget as a foundation, you can now start to make strategic decisions based on your goals.

Issa WHOLE Budget

CHECK THIS OUT!

You Can't Have it All. PRIORITIZE.

Quick Tip: If you are having trouble categorizing/prioritizing your expenses, consider classifying your expenses as either non-discretionary or discretionary.

Non-discretionary expenses are the ones that you incur every month and that are needed to survive (i.e.: food, rent, transportation, etc.). Discretionary expenses are things you want *after* your needs are cared for. You can also consider using numbers to prioritize your discretionary expenses, for example, 1-10 or 1-15, with 1 being the most important. Doing this will give you a clear picture of where your values and priorities lie AFTER your basic needs are met. This way, when it comes time to cut expenses, it's a simpler process to look at the least ranked items to see where you can cut.

For example, many people's top 5 list include expenses such as tithes, food, rent/mortgage, utilities, and car expenses. Least ranked items could be Netflix, eating out, or clothing. There is no right or wrong answer, because rankings are

> not a moral judgment, they simply represent what's most important to you.

Step 4: Create margin

In this context, margin is the difference between your income and your expenses. For example, if your income is $10 and your expenses are $8, you now have a margin of $2 because $10-$8=$2. All of your goals should involve some form of margin, because it is the way you create room in your budget to allocate money to said goals.

Why is margin important? Because you cannot pay down debt, save up for a vacation, make future investments, send money back home, or any planning without having some "cushion" in your finances in the form of margin. Ask yourself, do you have money from 2010? 2012? How about 2018? Part of it could be that you have not been able to live enough within your means to create margin in order to save some of that money from 10 years ago. You need this in order to move ahead and there are three ways to do so: decrease spending, increase income, or do both.

Once you are done setting up your bucket items in your budget and start to plan for the following month, look at places where you can make cuts in expenses. If you are tight on money, have huge debt and want to get ahead with your finances, go through your budget and cut out expenses, such as Netflix, that are nice to have, but may not be *absolutely* necessary, or are lower priority for you. (See quick tip on prioritizing discretionary expenses). Or, perhaps a high cost item is eating out, so instead, consider cooking in a more cost effective way. Gym memberships are also a common item that most people can cut if they don't use it enough to justify the expense.

It's common for immigrants to send money to family outside the country on a regular basis to help. While this is a valuable and noble gesture, this should really be practiced in a sustainable way that you can afford, and allows you to take care of your basic needs. Otherwise, it is martyrdom. I mention this because if you find yourself not being able to pay your rent and needing to cut expenses in order to create margin, consider sending less money for that month, or several months, until you are able to afford it again. Ultimately, your expenses need to reflect your values, but from time to time, we need to recalibrate our priorities to make sure we take care of ourselves before others. If not, we may not be able to care for those we love in the future.

One problem that is ubiquitous is that a lot of people live above their means. Someone who makes $50k a year using credit cards to live a lifestyle that is suited for someone making $85k/year is not conducive to long-term financial success. Even if that person with a $50k income has expenses totaling $50k a year, they are still living above their means, because they still have to deduct taxes, insurance, savings, retirement, and other expenses. So that person may need to live more of a $35k lifestyle. According to a research project by PYMENTS, "54% of consumers live paycheck to paycheck, including 53% of those who earn $50,000 to $100,000 a year." Even those living within their means can experience a devastating financial event, should unexpected expenses pop-up, i.e., the need to repair a car, health expenses, etc. Though an emergency fund (more on this later) could help soften the blow during such an unexpected event, living paycheck to paycheck is not an advisable strategy for the long-term.

Creating margin can be an extremely difficult process for some, because it involves sacrificing some wants and luxuries. If you choose not to create margin, then simply put, you will end up where you always have been, because it is extremely rare to have a good financial state without intention, planning, and sacrifice. Furthermore, you are telling yourself that your current situation is not bad enough for you to make any changes. So, if you'd like to meet your financial goals, cut unnecessary expenses out of your budget, increase income if you can, set those long-term goals, and allocate accordingly.

CHECK THIS OUT!

Can't Fill A Budget On Crumbs

It is important to acknowledge that while creating margin is crucial to getting ahead, wages in the United States have been stagnant for over 30 years, which makes it difficult for many people to make enough money for living expenses. Meaning, most people are working hard, but just aren't making enough money through no fault of their own. Minimum wage laws are exploitative, and this is in large part due to the influence that business leaders have over politicians. Even those not working a minimum wage job are still exploited as a result of an intentionally created environment that discourages unionization and collective bargaining, which, in turn, doesn't allow employees to negotiate their fair share of company profits; in addition to the Reagan era trickle down monetary policy that mostly benefits the richest citizens.

According to the U.S. Census, 54% of African Americans/Black communities reside south of the United States, with most people concentrated in AL, MS, FL, TX, LA, GA, VA, MD, NC, and SC. Excluding MD, the other nine states have a minimum wage below $9. These states also have the lasting impact of Jim Crow, which limited Black people's access to capital and income, and created an almost permanent underclass caste. This is something to keep in mind, that as a Black immigrant living in these states, it can be even more challenging to make enough money as a result of these lingering systemic discrimination.

Up north, Black immigrants are overly represented in urban centers like NYC, DC, and MI, which have a higher cost of living.

Consequently, even if you don't work in a minimum wage job, the cost of living in some of these cities can still make it very difficult to save money. Immigrants are likely to work a food service job, based on tips, as 40% of people who work at a tipped minimum wage job are minorities and immigrants. The tipped minimum wage is $2.13, meaning the employee is paid $2.13/hour, and hopefully can make enough money in tips to live. There are examples of employees making over $100,000 a year working on tips. However, this is eclipsed by the overwhelming amount of people who are exploited by being paid a $2.13 wage while living off very few tips – not to mention tipped employees can sometimes be responsible for fees to the employer which cuts even more into their income.

The Racial History of Tipping

According to Politico, "**Tipping originated in feudal Europe** *and was imported back to the United States by American travelers eager to seem sophisticated. The practice spread throughout the country after the Civil War as U.S. employers, largely in the hospitality sector, looked for ways to avoid paying formerly enslaved workers. Several states sought to end the practice in the early 1900s, often in recognition of its racist roots. But the restaurant industry*

> *fought back and was powerful enough to roll back local bans on tipping. And tipped workers—along with most others, as the act applied to industries that together made up only one-fifth of the labor force—were* **excluded** *from the first, limited federal minimum wage law passed in 1938."*

Step 5: Build your emergency fund

The first thing you should do once you build margin (difference between your income and expenses) is to use the excess cash acquired to build an emergency fund. An emergency fund helps to protect yourself and your household, should an unexpected emergency expense happen. I cannot overestimate the importance of having this cushion. Normally, I would recommend having 4-5 months' worth of living expenses (based on your budget) tucked away in a savings account to serve as your emergency fund and ready to go at a moment's notice. But for Black immigrants, I recommend having a goal of 6-8 months' worth of living expenses as emergency savings, especially if they are a first generation immigrant. I say goal because it is something to aim for, and once you reach your goal, you can start to redirect your savings to your other goals.

The reason I recommend 6-8 months is because, typically, first generation immigrants tend to have more risk and responsibilities. Meaning, they must take care of themselves and assist financially in taking care of their immediate family in the U.S. or back home. As a result, the working immigrant tends to be spread thinner, hence increasing their risk. Having several months of cushion allows you to be prepared in case there is loss of employment, a medical emergency or an expensive life event. Other factors, such as not having a job with benefits, or having children, add to your risk, and should be considered when establishing a goal for an emergency fund. Ultimately, it is up to you, your goals, your income, and a lot of other factors in determining what is obtainable for an emergency fund.

Setting up a solid emergency fund prior to other ventures, such as investing, makes sense for most people in the long term. For example, it is not advantageous to make investments before saving, in case you need to liquidate those very investments 2-3 months later, because there is an emergency $500 car repair. Or, using your extra money to pay your debt, only to find yourself in more debt once an emergency happens because you didn't have enough money saved up. If you are honest with yourself, "emergencies" come up somewhat often, and you need to be ready for them. In fact, some of these "emergencies" are actually recurring payments that you forget about and they sneak up on you. These can be budgeted for, but in the instance that you forgot about them, having an emergency fund can help you stay on track with your long-term goals. As you can see, for the most part, it makes sense to prioritize using your additional margin to establish a solid emergency fund.

> ## CHECK THIS OUT!
>
> **<u>Who Has Resilience?</u>**
>
> According to a survey from Bankrate.com, about 51% of Americans have less than three months of expenses saved up in an emergency fund. That total includes "25% having no emergency fund at all." Considering that this is a known problem in our current economy, it is important for us to proactively take the proper steps to do better as immigrants as we tend to carry more responsibilities and face more financial risks.

Once you have built up your emergency fund to match your goal, you can then start directing that amount to your other goals such as investments, debt, etc. In the instance that you have a goal of saving 6 months or more of living expenses, for example your living expenses are $2k per month, and you have saved a total of more than $12k ($2k * 6months = $12k) in your account, consider putting additional savings into an account that allows you to earn some return. Accounts such as a high yield savings account, or even a money market, can be good options for putting funds in excess of 6 months. It may also make sense for you to put that money under your mattress or in the stock market. Ultimately, your financial plan needs to fit your lifestyle, values, and long-term goals, so do your research, and choose what is best for you.

The point of an emergency fund is really not about growth, but about the preservation of capital. It is better for the money to be available at a moment's notice than to risk those funds in investments just for a higher return. Again, it is absolutely possible to invest your emergency fund, make a high return, and still maintain your funds. But, having an emergency fund is not about returns, it is about managing risk.

Issa WHOLE Budget

Sample Budget With Actuals

Monthly Budget		
Budgeted Income		Actual Income
Job 1	$1,000	
Job 2	$800	
Job 3	$200	
Total income	$2,000	$2,000
Budgeted Expenses		Actual Expenses
Car	$400	
Rent	$800	
Cell phone	$100	
Entertainment	$300	
Savings	$200	
Total Expenses	$1,800	$1,950
Net Income	$200	$50

- Best practice is to have a net income of $0 to make sure that every dollar is allocated towards an expense or goal. In the example, the $200 can be allocated to any of your other goals.

- Having a budget with an 'Actuals' column allows you to compare your budgeted expenses to what your actual expenses are once you are finished tracking them. This helps to plan for next month's budget with more information on what your actual spending needs are.

Key Takeaways:

1. A budget is a plan for how you will spend your money
2. Treat yourself with kindness and patience; your financial journey is a long process
3. Start simple and create expense buckets for your budget
4. Track your expenses and compare actual spending to budgeted spending
5. Create margin
6. Build an emergency fund with that margin (6-8 months is recommended

Creating Your Safety Nets

How to ensure your long-term well-being by creating financial safety nets.

Trent Gillies, in the *CNBC* article, "Why healthcare costs are making consumers more afraid of medical bills than an actual illness" mentions, "The poll, conducted by the University of Chicago and the West Health Institute, found Americans fear large medical bills more than they do serious illness. The data showed 33 percent of those surveyed were 'extremely afraid' or 'very afraid' of getting seriously ill." This, unfortunately, is very common, and speaks to the precarious economic conditions many people in the U.S. live under.

A safety net helps to provide stability during uncertain financial hardship. Broadly speaking, the U.S. lacks a robust, equitable, and accessible social safety net—especially when one's location and immigration status is considered. This means, depending on where you live and your immigration status, you may be at a higher risk of experiencing severe hardship due to a bad financial situation or decision. In this chapter, we will break down the importance of having a safety net, the different types of safety nets, and what they mean in the context of living in the United States.

Federal, State and Employer Based Safety Nets

For most people to have their basic needs met, they need to produce a good or service in return for money. If, for some reason, they cannot produce a good or service in return for money and have run out of funds and credit cards, other debt options are leveraged. This, however, is not sustainable, and may be followed by delinquent bills and going without necessities, such as food. To combat this, unemployment benefits, public shelters, and food stamps are in place to provide a cushion for people experiencing hard financial times to get the help they need. These programs, for the most part, work very well for the people that they reach, allowing them to get help while they find employment or a more sustainable way of living. These assistance programs may differ state by state, but are effective when well-funded and organized. The question now becomes; who has access to these safety nets, and how can you make sure your personal safety nets are in place?

Currently, many businesses depend on low wage contractors, or part-time workers who don't have full-time employee status. This allows employers to avoid paying for benefits, and keeps their employee expenses low. It also doesn't allow for those low wage workers to have the previously mentioned safety nets that normal employee status would give them. According to the Urban Institute, "This creates tension for the social safety net, because most of the nation's social policies, such as health insurance, unemployment insurance, and pensions are based on the traditional employer-employee relationship. Since immigrants are more likely to work these low wage jobs, they are more susceptible to not having a safety net in terms of savings, and will also lack access to government programs. More employers are contracting out whole areas of business (e.g. janitorial services or food preparation)," and this is where many first generation immigrants are likely to work.

Creating Your Safety Nets

CHECK THIS OUT!

Additional Supporting Information:

In 2017, 21.8% of African American households, and 18% of Latinx households reported food insecurity, while the national food insecurity rate was 11.8%. Black people are disproportionately impacted by the criminal system, face discrimination in hiring, have a greater prevalence of trigger events, such as a job loss or hospitalization, and any associated insurance loss. These happenings create economic instability and vulnerability that directly impact food security.

Examples of government funded safety nets:

- Employer benefits, combined with government programs, help to create social safety nets, including unemployment insurance that helps people who are out of work.

- Social Security, employer retirement, and Medicare help those in retirement.

- Workers compensation and disability insurance help those injured on the job.

Creating Your Safety Nets

- Paid leave from employers allows workers flexibility when they are sick, or to attend to the needs of a family member.

- Tax credits and public assistance provide income support to those whose incomes are low.

- Supplemental Nutrition Assistance Program (SNAP, commonly referred to as "food stamps") provides resources to buy food.

- Supplemental Security Income (SSI) provides cash assistance for seniors, individuals who are blind, and individuals with disabilities.

- The Temporary Assistance for Needy Families (TANF) program provides cash and noncash (child care, transportation, etc.) assistance for families with children.

- Public or subsidized housing provides assistance to pay for housing.

- Special Supplemental Nutrition Program for Women, Infants, and Children (WIC) provides food, nutrition education and counseling, and referrals for other social

Creating Your Safety Nets

> services to children, women who are pregnant, breastfeeding, or postpartum.
>
> - Child care subsidies through the Child Care and Development Fund (CCDF) program help pay for child care for families with children under age 13, and families with children under age 18 who have special needs.

While the aforementioned safety nets that are established through employment and through government programs work very well, it's evident that they are precarious in their current state, and even more so when we adjust for location and immigration status. The United States does not have an equitable social welfare system on a macro scale. What this means for most Black immigrants is that they must create alternative and numerous layers of safety nets that allow them to essentially be...human.

According to the Brookings Institution,

> "The principal government programs assisting those with low cash income are the Supplemental Nutrition

Assistance Program (SNAP, once called Food Stamps), Supplemental Security Income (SSI), and Unemployment Insurance (UI). Although SNAP and SSI rolls expand during periods of economic distress, benefits are low relative to most workers' earnings, and asset tests mean that most of the newly jobless are ineligible for SSI benefits and in some states for SNAP."

According to the 2021 article by the Urban Institute,

"Beyond eligibility restrictions, concerns around immigration status factor into immigrants' decisions to participate in public programs for which they or a family member may be eligible. Despite the hardships they faced during the pandemic, more than 1 in 4 adults in immigrant families with low incomes (27.5 percent) reported that they or a family member avoided noncash benefits or other help with basic needs because of immigration concerns in 2020."

Creating Your Safety Nets

The public safety programs are there, and they actually work very well. The issue, as with most public programs, is that they are not funded as much as they should be in order to meet the demands. Additionally, several barriers, such as eligibility based on immigration status and income exist that don't allow those who need it the most to benefit from it. This is part of the reason we live in a very fragile system.

Some immigrants may be disqualified from US citizenship for participating in a federal welfare/public good program, even if they pay taxes. The ruling, known as Public Charge, is nuanced, and is used by immigration officials to determine if you *may* become a public charge in the future, i.e., reliant on government assistance to survive. Always consult an immigration attorney when making decisions that may affect your immigration status.

CHECK THIS OUT!

Estate Planning:

Safety nets, such as life insurance and estate planning are important for protecting your family when you pass away. A 2022 *Blavity* article by Brickson Diamond titled, "How Black Americans Are Missing Out On The Largest Wealth Transfer In History" mentions, "An estate plan ensures your medical, financial, and guardianship decisions will be handled by the person(s) you choose and trust. Your plan ensures you have an advocate acting on your behalf, carrying out your wishes and directions as you intended." It is recommended that everyone over the age of 18 create an estate plan. This is an important step to ensure that your wealth is passed on properly to future generations. The same article mentions, "Over the next 25 years, an estimated $68 trillion will be transferred from U.S. households to heirs and charity. Not having a plan in place leaves many families in trouble as they struggle to manage the assets of their loved ones who have passed. "

According to Jenkins Fenstermaker, PLLC, "A US citizen with assets in the US may be able to develop a

Creating Your Safety Nets

relatively uncomplicated estate plan. The same is not necessarily true for immigrants. Immigration status, whether or not combined with owning assets in various countries, can complicate the estate planning process drastically. A non-US citizen wishing to develop an estate plan needs experienced guidance on how to meet his or her estate planning goals and manage the legal and tax ramifications for after-death transfers." Jenkins-Fenstermaker also shares that, "Three main factors for the development of a comprehensive estate plan:

i) The immigration status of the testator (the person creating the estate plan);

ii) The immigration status of the legatees or beneficiaries (the people inheriting any property or financial assets);

iii) The location of any financial accounts and property that is to be passed through the estate.

Durable power of attorney, healthcare power of attorney, and living will be documents that are involved in the process. Distribution of assets is a last will and testament that spells out who you want to give your assets to after you die. It also allows you to name a guardian for any minor children you may have."

CHECK THIS OUT!

American Exceptionalism

There is a mythology in the U.S. of "American exceptionalism." This is the belief that the U.S. is the best country on Earth, where anyone can achieve the "American Dream" (of course we know now this dream was never accessible to everyone). This belief system has created a doctrine that embraces capitalism and individualism. Right or wrong, this belief in American exceptionalism has caused many to reject any form of "social or universal" governance, especially for people of color as they are painted as lazy welfare queens stealing from the hardworking taxpayers. This racist rhetoric is not true. Since the end of the institution of slavery, many white Americans have violently opposed any policy that appeared to benefit exclusively or majority Black Americans. Under the New Deal, sectors that employed majority Black folks were not included in the language of the policy. The narrative of the lazy negro came along once Black Americans decided that they no longer wanted to be enslaved. This narrative

Creating Your Safety Nets

impacted policy so deeply that social safety net programs are viewed as entitlement programs.

Reagan's presidency was spent attacking the Civil Rights Act, which he and his southern delegation viewed as one big entitlement program. Despite being against their best interest, even poor whites supported Reagan's policies because they preferred economic oppression and maintaining their whiteness rather than being lumped in with Black people. Reagan rolled back civil rights laws and introduced the "welfare queen" to the public, which was a racist dog whistle term that signified the lazy Black woman on drugs who just lived off government assistance, despite there being no proof of this. In actuality, white citizens were and continue to be the biggest users of welfare. According to Business Insider, "A Department of Agriculture report from November estimated that 35.7% of SNAP recipients in the 2018 fiscal year were white, 25.1% were Black, 16.7% were Hispanic, 3% were Asian, and 1.5% were Native American." Since then, Democrats and Republicans have rolled back preexisting African American civil rights legislation and rebuked any national safety net program. Of course, the great irony in all of this is that socialism and welfare are practiced ubiquitously for the very wealthy individuals and

> corporations in the form of direct payments, tax benefits and favorable monetary policies (to name a few) not afforded to the public. The only difference is that they are labeled "government subsidies and bailout."

At any given point, living as a human being means that you will make mistakes and/or bad things will happen that negatively impact your finances. It is normal and somewhat expected that at some point you will get sick, there may be times you are unemployed, or things happen that are out of your control. In an ideal world, you would be able to use your savings or income to fix your problems. If these issues are compounded, meaning one bad event or decision happens after another, you will find that it can be very difficult to get back on your feet. According to MarketWatch, 56% of American consumers said they are living "paycheck to paycheck," and their life/stability hangs on by a thread. These people are at risk of a dire financial situation if any major health expense or house repair were to happen. Unfortunately, the current system in place does not give grace to that level of humanity and "life happening" (unless you have a certain level of privilege).

Personal Safety Nets

So, with all of this wahala around the lack of social safety nets, what can we do about it? First, I suggest having multiple layers of protection that include an ***emergency fund***, community support, insurance and strategic decision-making. There is no way to completely avoid financial setbacks, nor do I suggest that you can. The idea is to create financial resiliency against utter financial devastation when "life happens," because you would be able to tap into several layers of resources in order to support yourself and/or your family.

1. I discussed in the previous chapter the importance of having an emergency fund to use for unexpected expenses. Ideally, you would have at least 3-6 months of expenses in your account and use your budget to help you reach that goal. Having this layer of savings gives you peace of mind that if you were to lose your job, you will have at least 3-6 months to look for another one. If you are injured and can't work, this will buy you

some time, especially if you are uninsured or work a job with little to no benefits. Some people are fortunate enough to work for organizations that provide salary payments, or partial payments, even in the event of injury, but unfortunately, this is not the case for everyone. The more savings you have, the bigger your safety net will be.

CHECK THIS OUT!

Money Pool:

Many African/majority Black countries practice money sharing, which involves a group of committed individuals contributing money to a pool on a monthly basis and then one member gets a large sum each month. In the Caribbean, it's known as Partner and in Senegal, we call it Tontine. This allows individuals to avoid borrowing money from the bank (which would include interest), to fund family ventures, educational and business needs. This group is usually brought together based on shared values, trust, kinship, transparency, and strong communication.

Creating Your Safety Nets

2. Having a ***community*** can mean many things to different people, but the value that all these different communities have in common is that they can be depended on for support and to offer resiliency against a life event that may have otherwise resulted in a severe financial crisis. The idea behind community is that a group of people are able to pull their resources together for a common purpose all based on shared values. Those values can be based on the fact that all those people love to cook Jollof Rice (from Senegal of course) or it could be that all of those people are of a particular religion or maybe all those people love going out or playing futbol (AKA soccer) together. There are so many different types of communities that you can be a part of, and they are all valid.

Ideally, if there was a time where you would need help, you would depend on that community. They may not be able to solve all of your problems, but with each person chipping in for a car ride, or even $5, it can make a world of difference. When COVID initially hit, I had several members of my community lose their jobs; nonetheless, because we were in the same community I was able to fundraise $25-$30 from people that I knew, and we were able to send thousands of dollars in funds in a matter of 4 hours. The power of community is tremendous because everyone has something to contribute–which doesn't always have to be money–when you need them the most. Time, emotional support, or even information sharing are ways a community can help besides spending money.

One thing that is important when it comes to community is that you must invest in your community, especially when others are in need. As mentioned earlier, the value of shared resources and collectivism is one thing I absolutely love about my Senegalese/African culture and that is something at play here as well. Again, the goal is to have a layer of resiliency when life happens and a community, no matter what it looks like, can be tremendously powerful in enabling that because most if not all those people are able and willing to help one another.

3. The value of ***insurance*** (if you get the right kind) is that it can protect you from high

Creating Your Safety Nets

costs later down the line when an unexpected life event occurs. It does this by putting you in a pool with other individuals who are looking for the same protection but have higher or lower risk than you. However, it is important that you get insurance that makes sense for you and your lifestyle and not waste money on insurance you don't need. I won't go into detail of every single type of insurance because that is not my goal. Instead, I would like to point out the value of having insurance in general and why you should consider different types of coverage based on *your* lifestyle. For example, having car insurance (besides the fact that it's mandatory in some states) will protect you from high costs in the event of an accident.

As an immigrant in general, I think it's always a good rule of thumb to avoid exposure to risk and the court systems. Whether or not your green card is in process, or you have a student visa, ideally you want to give immigration as well as the U.S. government as little adverse material against you as possible—especially considering that the U.S. justice system penalizes Black people at higher and more severe rates than white people. Having car insurance is one way of protecting yourself.

Other common types of insurance are property insurance in the case of a fire, flooding or burglary; rental insurance that covers expenses in the event that there is damage to the property or your possessions while you are renting.

The elephant not only in the room but the whole country is health insurance. (Sigh*) I will start by saying the U.S has one of, if not the most inefficient health care systems in the world, and one that is meant to create high profits for certain stakeholders while leaving patients to pay high costs. I say this because more than likely you will find the journey of taking care of health costs challenging if not impossible. But you can still find a plan that works for you.

According to healthcare.gov, generally speaking most health insurance plans allow individuals younger than 26 to be covered by their parent's job-based plan. This can vary state to state and plan by plan but if one qualifies, it could be a huge money saver. According to the National

Creating Your Safety Nets

Immigration Law Center, non-applicants to the Affordable Care Act (ACA) do *not* need to provide their citizenship or immigration status when applying to get health insurance for their eligible family members. Each member of a mixed-status family may be eligible for a different health care program and some members may not be eligible for comprehensive health care coverage. In general, citizens and "lawfully present" immigrants are eligible to buy health insurance and get tax-credit subsidies in the health care marketplaces created under the ACA. However, people who have Deferred Action for Childhood Arrivals (DACA) are excluded from the marketplaces. Undocumented immigrants also are not eligible to buy health insurance and receive subsidies from the ACA marketplaces. States have different rules about immigrants' eligibility for Medicaid and the Children's Health Insurance Program (CHIP), but eligibility is generally limited to a subset of lawfully present immigrants called "qualified" immigrants.

CHECK THIS OUT!

Okay, Story Time!

When I was in college, I found myself with chest pains on the last day of the semester. It took me a total of 5 days of not being able to breathe or walk very far before I decided to take the bus and check myself into the hospital because I lived under the pretense that the only reason I have to see a doctor is if I was dying. My reluctance in going to the doctor was because I was well aware of the cost of visiting one.

After being admitted, I saw 11 doctors in a matter of 6 hours. After many tests, I was finally told that the chest pains and lack of breathing were not due to my heart like I suspected. I had a collapsed left lung, which is known as pneumothorax. I was very surprised as I had a 1/200,000 chance of this happening to me. I was told that had I not come in, it could have been much much worse. A week later, I was hit with five different envelopes that came into the mail with a total charge of more than $3,500! This is a lot of money now, but especially when I was in college. Keep in mind that I had no operations

Creating Your Safety Nets

done, just testing, and I was told to breathe in a tube.

I tell this story to say that every year people avoid going to the doctor or taking their medicine because they fear the cost of health care. This can and does result in death. So, it is important that if you are able–you choose the right health insurance, especially because they vary, and it is important to do your due diligence when making these decisions. If you do not qualify for health insurance through employment or the government, reach out to local nonprofits, local county governments or even community groups for resources. If you are lucky, you may be able to get health services in certain clinics that deal with low income or out of status individuals. Don't hesitate and don't be ashamed to access these resources either. The U.S. has millions of citizens who are not able to see a dentist for a toothache, because they are financially insecure and cannot afford to pay $3,200 just to have a tooth taken out. Don't risk your health. If you need help, go see a doctor and the worst thing that could happen is that they will report your unpaid medical bills to the credit bureaus, which isn't so bad considering that your life may be saved.

Insurance Types

Please note that there are many more types of insurance outside of the ones listed below. I've included the ones that I think are most commonly used and are important to be aware of. I encourage you to do your research and determine which insurance type and terms are best for you.

Insurance Type	Description
Life Insurance	There are a wide variety of life insurance policies. The most basic— and least expensive—is term life insurance, which pays a specific amount out to your beneficiaries if you die within the timeframe of the policy.
Health Insurance	Helps to cover health related expenses. This is highly recommended as the costs of healthcare are often astronomical.

Creating Your Safety Nets

Car Insurance	Automobile insurance pays for repairs and health care (depending on the terms) in the event that you experience a car wreck, and it will also pay for the other party's damages if you are at fault.
Disability Insurance	This type of coverage is intended to replace your salary if you were to become temporarily or permanently disabled.
Long-term Care Insurance	This insurance helps cover costs in the event that you need to be in nursing care, either on a short- or a long-term basis. You should also consider whether you have assets outside the policy that could pay for your care. If not, strong coverage may be more necessary for your family.
Homeowners Insurance	Homeowners insurance pays for partial damage or the complete destruction of your home. It often covers the damaged contents of your home, as well as the funds

	necessary to rent other accommodations while your home is being repaired.
Liability Insurance	Liability insurance is often attached to your homeowners' policy, and it covers accidents that may happen at your home. For example, if a house guest slipped on your stairs, you might be responsible for their medical expenses if you were found liable for the accident. Liability coverage would mitigate those costs.

4. Lastly, when it comes to building resiliency there is nothing like making good ***strategic decisions*** on a daily basis. Overall, your future self and life is a result of the day to day decisions you make and oftentimes it's not about making the right decision but focusing on the thinking process used in making those decisions. Take the time to reflect on *how* you decide to purchase things that you like. Let's say you are walking in the market, and you see someone selling suya,

Creating Your Safety Nets

what is the thought process in your head that may lead you to buy some suya or ignore the suya? Whatever it is, it's not right or wrong. Every spending decision means you are giving up one thing in exchange for another thing, which has its advantages and disadvantages. When it comes to building resiliency and reducing the risk of a life event bringing you into deep poverty, your day to day decisions are where you lay the foundation to create a strong margin that will help you survive a major life event.

Personally, I love Aldo shoes, and for some reason, every time I go to a store, I have a strong urge to buy a pair of shoes. My thought process when this urge comes is; #1, do I have the money saved up for it? My budget answers that question. #2, is this something I need right *now*? #3, how *often* will I use it or how many outfits can I rock it with? Asking myself these three simple questions helps me make smart spending decisions and for these decisions I leave my emotions out of it—no matter how much it pains me. I once waited on a pair of boots for 13 months because I could not sufficiently answer all three of these questions. Am I

Creating Your Safety Nets

perfect? No! I once purchased two Aldo shoes completely unplanned for. I was weak. But we all have our weak moments, and I was able to learn from it. Oftentimes, people make purchases based on their emotions and how much they like something, which is fine. But after the emotions scream at you, your brain then needs to kick in and rationalize that purchase.

For example, it might not make sense for you to buy a luxury SUV in NYC when you don't even have parking and you travel faster with the subway. Although you may love the car, you will not get as much utility from it. It is good practice to make sure that purchases will be used enough times to justify their existence and that goes for all purchases, but *especially* for big purchases. In the context of the U.S, consumerism can consume you into making purchases that may not make sense for you and your lifestyle. Remember, your financial life is unique to you, and you should not make spending decisions trying to impress others if it doesn't make financial sense because those very people judging you will not be paying your rent or mortgage when it's delinquent. Consumerism

Creating Your Safety Nets

also says that the more money you make, the higher your standard of living should be. This means that someone making $100 spends $100 and when they make $1,000 they spend $1,000 and then have to work even harder to keep up with the lifestyle they created. This is called lifestyle inflation and at its best it's unhealthy, at its worst it's destructive.

You must live below your means in order to create margin in your budget, so you can increase your savings and fortify your personal safety net. So, if you are making $100 and then you start making $300, keep living like you were making that $100 and put the rest towards your long-term goals. This does not mean hoarding your money. In fact, what this means is that you can be more generous with your money, because you can better plan where it's being allocated. This also doesn't mean cutting costs to a point where your basic needs (food, housing, etc.) are not being met. You should absolutely make sure you have food, housing, and clothes to have a decent life. This also doesn't mean you can't have nice things. What it means is having nice things may take a little more patience and planning to make sure those very nice things don't become a burden or your breaking point in the long run.

> **CHECK THIS OUT!**
>
> <u>All Safety Nets Aren't Created Equal</u>
>
> The 1996 federal welfare reform law introduced a more conservative stance on who is eligible for welfare benefits and reduced the amount or duration of the benefits. Temporary Assistance to Needy Families (TANF) is a federally funded program with strict work first mandates and zero tolerance policies that cause families to lose all TANF benefits upon their first program violation.
>
> A student's citizenship status or lack thereof can prevent them from ever receiving federal assistance. They may be eligible for state funding, but most student financial aid packages are bolstered by federal money. This dramatically decreases potential money for higher education, which may lead to more debt. Undocumented students, including DACA recipients, are not eligible for federal student aid, but may still be eligible for state or college aid, in addition to private scholarships. According to Higher Ed Immigration Portal (a platform that integrates

Creating Your Safety Nets

data, policy analysis, and resources to support DACA and undocumented, refugee, other immigrant, and international students.), the U.S. is home to more than 427,000 undocumented students, including DACA recipients, in higher education. Each state implements its own policies in terms of providing access to in-state tuition and state financial aid to the state's undocumented residents. Some states, such as California, DC, Maryland, and New York, provide Comprehensive Access which are statewide policies that provide access to in-state tuition, some state financial aid or scholarships for the state's resident DACA recipients and undocumented students. To find out your state's category visit www.higheredimmigrationportal.org/states/.

You may find that while many people experience poverty, getting out of it can be heavily impacted by the color of your skin. Getting out of poverty is oftentimes harder for Black people because the traditional ways of doing so (employment, government assistance, and education) are restricted due to the impact of racism and poverty. Additionally, financially vulnerable Black families are more likely to experience eviction in their lifetime. The eviction impacts their ability to secure another rental property and should they

> seek to buy a home, the eviction could increase the chances of a home loan denial.

Key Takeaways:

- Having safety nets in place are crucial for long-term peace of mind

- Savings: Your first line of defense against financial devastation should be having an emergency fund with a minimum of 3-6 months' worth of your expenses

- Community/relationships: Being in community based on shared values can be a powerful layer of protection to receive and give help

- Insurance: The right insurance can lower major unplanned costs

- Strategic Decision-Making: Your decision-making process is very important because today's good decisions determine your future

Getting Out of Debt

Now, if you find yourself in debt either with credit cards, auto or student loans, or all of the above, the good news is that you can get out of your debt. The bad news is, depending on how high the debt is, it will require a lot of discipline and sacrifice to do that. However, debt isn't all bad. According to CNBC, "'Good' debt is defined as money owed for things that can help build wealth or increase income over time, such as student loans, mortgages or a business loan. 'Bad' debt refers to things like credit cards or other consumer debt that do little to improve your financial outcome. These are oversimplifications. The distinctions between 'good' and 'bad' debt are a lot more nuanced."

Debt, especially large bad debt such as store credit cards, are one of those things that can severely stagnate your financial progress simply because it takes a portion of your monthly revenue in the form of repayments. This is made worse especially during recessions where you may lose your job or during times of high inflation where the costs for items such as groceries increase, but you still need to make debt payments. If you're in need of margin, getting rid of bad debt should be a priority to create room in your monthly budget so your money is going towards your goals, such as that Cancun vacation trip and not your Macy's credit card.

The core of your debt reduction strategy should be to create enough margin by leveraging your budget and paying it down as much as possible. As mentioned, a budget is simply a plan for how you will spend your money and more importantly a reflection of your values. Additionally, I mentioned previously the importance of having an emergency fund before making aggressive payments to your debt because unexpected life events can happen. This will allow you to avoid going into more debt if/when an emergency pops up. While you are building up your emergency fund, one strategy you can use is making minimum payments to all of your debts, so as to not increase your principal balance (always read your debt agreement carefully and understand the policies as they may differ, and this may not apply to you). Once you have reached your

Getting Out of Debt

emergency fund goal, you can now start to divert future monthly savings into aggressively paying down your debt.

For example, let's say you have an emergency fund goal of $6,000 and you save $600/month. After 10 months, you would have saved up your goal of $6,000 ($600*10months = $6,000) and you would then start to divert this $600 monthly savings into paying off your credit card. This is the ideal scenario; however, we don't live in a perfect world and what's likely to happen is that some months you can put away $600, other months $100 and some months $700. Expect this to flow as you adjust to life in general. Additionally, this is not a hard and fast rule, but more of a general guidance. Meaning, if it makes more sense for you and your life not to wait 10 months to start making aggressive payments to your debt then you should do that. Ultimately, you are in charge of your financial life and because we all have a financial picture as unique as our fingerprints, you have to decide what fits best within your situation.

CHECK THIS OUT!

Debt Consolidation

Debt consolidation is a form of debt refinancing that entails taking out one loan to pay off others. Debt consolidation is a common strategy used to reduce monthly debt payments by combining different types of debt into one that has the lowest interest rate.

For example, let's say you have the below debts:

- Credit card #1: balance is $10, interest rate of 8%
- Credit card #2: balance is $10, interest rate of 6%
- Credit card #3: balance is $10, interest rate of 3%

In the example above, consolidation would look like using credit card #3 to pay off credit cards #1 and #2. Why? Because, although all three cards have the same balance, credit card #3 has the lowest interest rate; therefore, you would be paying less money over time. After using credit card #3 to pay off #1 and #2, #3 would now have a balance of $30 at a 3% interest rate. This also assumes that credit card #3 has a limit large enough that will allow you to pay off other debts. This does not have to be done with credit cards; there are other forms of debt consolidation, so make sure you choose what's right for you.

This tactic can be very helpful in helping people get out of debt faster. But, a common pitfall is that people sometimes go right back into debt after consolidating because they don't have (wait for it) *an emergency fund*. Let's say you consolidate your debt into one card and then an emergency car repair happens. Now, you may have to go into more debt with the same card or a different card, because you did not use the extra money saved with consolidation to build your emergency fund. It is absolutely crucial that you shield yourself as much as possible from taking on more debt when trying to get out of debt. And the best way to do so is to build up an emergency fund.

Strategies to tackling debt:

1. Debt snowball method: This is a phrase coined by the financial guru Dave Ramsey and the power behind this method is psychological momentum. This method suggests you first start making large payments to your debt with the smallest balance first. Then as you pay that off, snowball your way up and apply the same payment amounts to your second smallest debt until you eventually pay it off. The idea is that you will increase the size of the debt you tackle just as a snowball would increase in size as it rolls down the mountain collecting momentum.

For example, you have three debt balances: credit card: $200; laptop: $500; and car: $2,000 and you are making monthly payments of $50. The debt snowball method suggests that you apply these payments to the smallest balance, which in this case is the credit card. You would make aggressive payments and get rid of that $200 credit card debt first (while making minimum payments to the laptop and car to avoid an increase of your principal balance). Once the credit card debt has been fully paid off, take the $50 you were using to pay the credit card each month, in addition to any spare money, and apply it to your laptop debt until that's paid off. And finally, move on to the car. This method works really well because seeing debt paid off creates a reward for your brain and provides you with momentum and motivation to keep going.

Furthermore, because you started with the smallest debt first, you won't have to wait too long to experience that feeling of success and dopamine, which leads to being able to build that psychological momentum. It's important that with the debt snowball method you are *aggressive* with your payments. This means that while creating your budget, you should allocate less funds to *elective* things such as eating out or shopping for clothes in order to viciously attack the debt and pay it off as fast as you possibly can without neglecting your basic needs.

a. Advantage: It allows for psychological momentum especially for those who need more motivation. Consequently, people are more likely to stick with the plan.

b. Disadvantage: Over time, you will pay slightly more because you are not focusing on the highest interest rate first. It also requires sacrificing some wants in order to get out of debt quicker.

2. Avalanche method: The second strategy is focused on paying the debt with the highest

interest first. Mathematically speaking, paying down your debt from highest to lowest interest rate means you pay slightly less over time because you are getting rid of the highest rate first.

For example, if we take the same three examples but now assume the following interest rates: credit card: 13%; laptop: 18%; car: 22%. With this method, you would start making aggressive payments on the *car* first because it has the highest interest rate of 22% out of the three debt balances, while making minimum payments on the laptop and credit card to avoid an increase in your principal balances. Since the car has the highest interest rate, the cost savings will be higher if you pay it off first. Also consider the percentage of the interest rate and the balance of the debts when choosing which debt to pay off first. For example, having a $500 debt with a 20% interest has the same interest accrual as having a $5,000 debt balance with a 2% interest. So always choose what makes the most sense for you.

a. Advantage: Mathematically, it is the most cost effective way to pay down debt.

b. Disadvantage: Doesn't allow you to build psychological momentum and can take longer to see results, which can cause people to quit prematurely and give up on the goal.

3. Pay your debt: I don't mean to oversimplify this but if you have the money, pay it off. There are many people who have debt, but also have significant amounts of liquidity (cash) and would rather not pay down that debt for one reason or another. As mentioned, a huge part of personal finance is psychological, and some people would rather not see a large sum of money drained from their account. In this case, you need to make a calculated decision. Meaning, if you have an emergency fund and margin in your budget and you are able to pay off that $2,000 credit card balance, in most cases you should do it.

I always encourage people to have an individual analysis based on their unique scenario. So, if you can afford it, pay that balance, and get that debt out of the way so you can focus on a better future. Don't let a false sense of security like having that $2k in savings stop you from planning for your future. Whether you are planning a vacation, buying a car cash or saving up for Hajj, you can accomplish anything with proper planning and getting roadblocks like credit card debt out of the way. When you avoid paying off debt, you are simply prolonging the inevitable use of the money you have saved up.

CHECK THIS OUT!

<u>Loan Forgiveness, With a Catch</u>

One common way graduates consider getting rid of their student debt is by signing up for a federal student loan forgiveness program. These programs allow new employees to work for a federal agency or any approved program for a certain number of years, usually for low pay and following certain criteria with the hope of having their student loans wiped out. While this may be a good option for some, be wary of signing up for something you do not understand or may not be able to fully commit to. According to education.org, only "6.8% of applicants for federal student loan forgiveness have had the remainder of their student loan payments discharged. Some received letters of denial from the

> government after years in the program, wasting valuable time in a low paying job."

Lastly, with regards to paying debt, you have to decide whether the snowball method or the avalanche method works best for you or both. There are advantages and disadvantages to either approach. But it's important to look at the bigger picture, which is that you will have a plan and no matter what you choose, it will get you to your ultimate goal of being debt free.

Key Takeaways:

- No matter how much debt you have, you can get out of it with the right plan
- Before getting out of debt, you must have an emergency fund
- Creating margin by leveraging your budget is the most effective weapon you can use to get out of debt

Getting Out of Debt

- Methods:
  - Snowball method allows psychological momentum and is most recommended
  - The avalanche method allows someone to pay their debt in the most mathematical sense
  - If you have the money, pay off your debts
  - Use a combination of both if one works better at a certain time in your life

Getting Into Debt

Debt plays a huge function in the American lifestyle, and many advise that in order to progress in life, you must leverage debt. (In this case, I am using the term "leveraging debt" to mean someone who borrows money from an institution and has to pay it back or their credit score will be affected). In reality, many people don't have the tools and skills to effectively manage the debt and find themselves on the losing end of that strategy.

Credit

Now, in order to leverage debt, you will need a good credit score. What is credit? Credit is the ability to borrow money with the understanding that you will pay it back later, most times with interest. The benefits of having credit, especially good credit, is that you get to borrow money often at a cheaper price or lower interest rate—this means you pay back less interest on the money you borrowed. This is useful when qualifying for a mortgage to buy a house or trying to get a credit card as well, because the better your credit the more favorable your terms will be.

In order to build credit, you must show a history of having access to credit and being able to pay it off in a timely manner. This tells the banks and other financial institutions that you are able to pay back borrowed money in a timely manner and therefore you can be trusted with their money.

Credit score calculation methods:

1) Payment history: to determine if you have paid past debt on time; late payment history will hurt your score

2) Credit line usage: to see how high is the credit amount that you are using compared to the total that you have access to; high debt to credit ratios can negatively impact your credit score

3) Credit history: to determine how long you have had lines of credit; longer credit history will positively impact your score

4) Credit mix: the different types of debt you have; diverse debt will have a positive impact on your score

Getting Into Debt

5) New credit: opening many credit lines in a short amount of time can hurt your credit

There are many ways to build credit, but the most popular ways are through having credit cards or a car loan. Two tactics that many people use to build credit (besides making sure they pay on time) are: to open credit cards but not use them; and calling the bank to extend their current limits, *without increasing their usage*.

According to WalletHub:

"When you have an open credit card account that you never use, the credit bureaus will merely see that you have available credit that you don't tap into. And that, of course, means that your credit utilization is low, indicating that you aren't desperate for credit to support your spending habits. In other words, it will fill your credit reports with information that reflects favorably upon your financial responsibility on a monthly basis and therefore help you build credit. For a zero balance credit card strategy to work, the card in question simply must not have an annual fee. Otherwise, you'll waste money while your account sits dormant. From a credit building standpoint, you're better off making purchases with a credit card and paying for them in full by the due date than you are not using the card at all. Making purchases with a credit card and proving yourself capable of paying the right amount at the proper time at least gives financial institutions a track record of credit utilization and payment on which to base their estimates for future performance."

According to U.S. World News, "The most dangerous risk of not using a card is that you might stop looking at your statements, too. Failing to monitor your account might leave you in the dark about fraudulent activity." Ultimately, you have to do what's right for you. If you can manage to pay back a credit card on time, then use it. But if you know that you are not organized enough, then don't.

From the five credit score calculation methods I listed above, these actions, if done right, can strengthen your credit score over time because the more access to credit you have without using it, the more you are proving to be a safe holder of capital and not desperate for the money. Word of caution, however, if you know your relationship with money is toxic and having access to that much capital will be more

Getting Into Debt

detrimental than good, I would suggest that you be less aggressive using this tactic, or not use it at all.

Consider someone like person (A) who has access to $10,000 on a credit card and uses $8,000 each month compared to another person (B) who has the same access of $10,000 but only uses $3,500. The banks and credit system look favorably on person (B) because they are only using 35% of their available credit ($3.5k/$10K= 35%) while person (A) is using 80% of their available credit ($8k/$10k=80%). Again, the story this tells is that person (A) is overextended and desperate for money and therefore more likely to default. This can hurt your score, so try to not use more than 35% of your available balance on your credit card if you can. Additionally, if person (A) called the bank to extend their limit to $20k instead of the $10k, their new usage rate would be down to 40% ($8k/$20k=40%) which is favorable to their score and helps to increase it over time.

I have personally decided not to participate in the credit system because it is not something that works for me and my lifestyle. The game of having to be in debt in order to take on more debt to prove you can handle the greatest debt is something that personally doesn't appeal to me (at this moment). I have had credit cards in the past, and I may change my mind in the future, but for the moment, I choose not to. This decision to not have a credit card has shocked many people because the overwhelming belief is that in order to be successful one must participate in the credit market. To their point, having good credit can help a lot if you ever need to lease a car or buy a house. But, I have made my decision. So do what's best for you.

Credit Cards

Credit card companies and other financial institutions are aware that most people don't have the tools to manage the debt they take on. Historically, many of these companies have taken advantage of this fact to make profits. In more recent times, some financial institutions have realized it's better to have an educated consumer base in the long-term rather than take advantage of them in the short-term.

Ideally, you would get a credit card, spend some of it and pay it off every month to build your credit over time. And that's the idea of the credit system; to have a trail of proof that you are able to reliably pay off debt month after month. The problem is many individuals don't have the skills to manage credit or their finances in general which leads them to massive debt that is hard to dig themselves out of. This can be *very* profitable for credit card companies.

Megan Dematteo shares on CNBC,

> "When making a decision about taking on more debt, you'll also want to think about where you are in life at this moment, and where you want to be several years from now. Someone in their 20s can arguably afford to take more risks when it comes to borrowing and investing, since they have more time to correct their course if they make a few mistakes along the way. But just because you can afford to take risks doesn't mean you should be all-out reckless. If you do decide to take on more debt, you should always have a plan to pay it off. And then stick to that plan." It is important to follow certain rules when engaging in debt

transactions, and even more importantly, know your relationship status with money and what you can handle. "The more money you borrow, the more you'll pay in interest charges and fees. Always review the interest rates on any kind of credit or loan product before you apply. Break it down into monthly, or even daily fees, to get perspective as to just how much your debt truly costs. Also look for hidden costs like origination fees, early payoff penalties, and more."

Knowing yourself goes a long way in deciding whether to take on debt. If you know that you have a spending problem, perhaps think twice about getting 4-5 credit cards with high interest rates and maximums. If you forget things or are not organized enough to make all the payments on time, then having 5 credit cards may not make sense. Many people are lured by the perks that credit cards offer, but you must do a calculation to make sure that the expenses are not more than the benefits. For example, it may not make the best sense to pay $400 in annual fees for a credit card with great travel rewards,

Getting Into Debt

if you are not someone who travels often. Or get a store credit card from JCPenney, Best Buy or Macy's if you do not shop at those locations frequently enough to justify the credit card fees. And sometimes life happens. Let's say you plan to take a trip, so you get a credit card with frequent flier miles and buy things that you would not have normally bought, just to get those perks and come to find out something like coronavirus hits and you can't fly, anyway. On top of that, you may be left with debt on the card that you can't repay. The bottom line is, think twice before signing up for a credit because banks don't give out free money and they are not in the business of charity, they are in the business of MAKING MONEY. According to Statista.com,

> "credit card companies spend millions advertising credit cards to consumers. These companies spend time getting to know the clientele's psyche, in hopes of being able to make an appealing offer to clients. Though, leveraging debt can be a good idea to build wealth, one should have a strategy in mind before embarking in such a venture. Again,

banks are in the business to make money." Don't be on the wrong side of the credit card game, but instead be clear about your relationship with money, why you want a credit card and have a plan for managing that credit card.

CHECK THIS OUT!

Black Debt Trap

Most Black Americans who find themselves in debt are actually employed. The problems of debt tend to be tied to generational poverty and the results of a systematic denial of economic resources. "The Challenge of Credit Card Debt for the African American Middle Class", co-authored by Demos and the NAACP reported that during difficult economic times, many Black families rely more on credit cards to make ends meet and make purchases. Black People are also more likely to pay higher interest rates and suffer more negative consequences of debt than other groups.

Mortgages

The Consumer Financial Protection defines a mortgage as "an agreement between you and a lender that allows you to borrow money to purchase or refinance a home."

More than likely, you have heard or been told that in order to move ahead in the U.S., build wealth, and have the American dream, you must not waste your money on rent and that you need to get a house through a mortgage. It is true that one of the best ways people in the U.S. have been able to generate wealth over time has been by purchasing real estate. The idea is that you buy a house now, and it will be worth more in the future, then you can sell it for a profit. In turn, having a home is oftentimes one of the most effective ways for people to build wealth as home prices can appreciate quickly given the right market conditions. However, buying a house has been romanticized in a very dangerous way because many believe they are guaranteed to succeed in it. This belief has resulted in many people finding themselves in a bad financial position as a result of not doing their homework. In reality, the house can surely be an asset but can also be a liability if not done correctly. Before deciding to buy a house, you

Getting Into Debt

must have adequate due diligence to make sure you can even afford a house.

One argument that is perpetuated is when people say that their rent money is a waste because that same amount could be spent on a mortgage to build equity. In this instance, let's say the rent payment is $1,200/month and the mortgage payment would also be $1,200. Oftentimes, this analysis is flawed because what's not considered is the annual maintenance cost that is usually an additional 1-3% of the purchase price. So that $1,200 payment may actually be $2,300/month depending on what may go wrong or needs fixing in the house. I could write a whole book on getting a mortgage, but that is not the focus of this one. Instead, my focus is to urge due diligence on the largest financial commitment most people will ever make. Due diligence looks like taking homeownership education courses, making sure your mortgage payment isn't more than 30%-38% of your monthly income, among other things.

> **CHECK THIS OUT!**
>
> Additional Insight:
>
> For those who choose not to participate in the credit system or in many cases with immigrants who cannot participate in the credit system, there is an alternative way of getting a mortgage without the use of credit scores. Some banks can do "manual underwriting" which is a hands-on investigation into your ability to repay debt. While this is a longer process and can be more strenuous, it's still possible to get a mortgage without a credit score. Additionally, some lenders will allow one individual with no credit score to get a mortgage loan with one or two other individuals who do have credit scores. You can also get a Federal Housing Administration (FHA) loan which qualifies borrowers with little to no credit, but these loans can be more expensive.

If you plan on getting a mortgage, consider paying as much as you can towards the down payment to get rid of the private mortgage insurance (PMI), although this option is not ideal for a lot of people. PMI is an extra payment that is required if you have a mortgage with a Loan to Value ratio that is more than 80% (that means you borrowed more than 80% of the value for the property). In other words, you need to make a down payment that is 20% or more of the home's purchase amount to avoid paying a PMI.

You may also consider saving up and buying your house in cash instead of getting a mortgage. The downside with this approach is that it may take several years to save up enough money to buy a house in cash, especially when you consider location, inflated prices due to low inventory, and stagnant wages. Time value of money is also a factor here. Over time, the value of the cash you hold diminishes (if not invested or growing in value) with inflation, especially if you are waiting 8-10 years to purchase a property, whereas with a loan you only use part of your money up front. The upside is buying a house in cash is cheaper in the long run, because interest payments are not involved as well as other fees associated with a mortgage. You also don't need to worry about any of the painful processes involved in getting a loan. Neither approach is right nor wrong, it is a matter of making the best decision for yourself.

CHECK THIS OUT!

Exclude Black Housing

A recent study and survey by the Fair Housing Council of Greater Washington sent Black and white applicants with the same exact economic profiles to banks to apply for loans. They discovered that brokers discussed loan fees with 74 percent of the white shoppers, but only 31 percent of the minority shoppers. Brokers discussed fixed-rate mortgages for first time borrowers with 90 percent of the white applicants, but just 56 percent of the minority applicants. Brokers spent an average of 39 minutes discussing loan options with white applicants, but only spent an average of 27 minutes with African American or Hispanic applicants.

This report demonstrated that simply having the right numbers and income do not prevent

> discriminatory loan practices, which outside of outright denying Black applicants also denies Black borrowers access to key cost saving information. We are denied the information needed to compare potential lenders and often feel stuck to the financial institution we started the application with.

Payday loans

A payday loan is a short-term unsecured loan, often characterized by high interest rates. This debt system can be and has been exploitative to many, especially the most vulnerable people in society who do not have the tools or skills to manage it. This can lead them to end up with thousands of dollars in debt, plus interest.

Payday loan companies typically target vulnerable populations that are low-income, immigrants, Black, white and everyone in between. At times, these payday companies can charge interest rates as high as 300%. Ideally, one would use a payday loan service and pay the money back with interest. The issue is these short-term payday loans attract those who have

Getting Into Debt

little to no option at times and may be desperate to fund short-term emergencies, such as buying food for their children or medicine. And so, the context in which these payday services work is oftentimes dubious and something you want to avoid. Some payday companies use draconian servicing practices that keep the debt in their books longer in order to earn more money. Therefore, these types of loans can end up being a debt trap for the borrowers, because they are not able to get out of their debt even after paying off their loans.

There may be some very good reasons to use a payday service, but it should be a last ditch measure. Try to avoid it at all costs. Consider the following as alternatives:

1. Ask family or friends for money
2. Sell assets, such as clothes, shoes, electronics
3. Form a lending circle
4. Check local non-profits/organizations who can help with your situation
5. Apply for a bank loan

6. Look for a job in the gig economy (Uber, delivering food, cleaning, repairing)

This scenario unfortunately does happen and can be debilitating to the spirit, the body and one's quality of life. And since credit can be used to determine employment eligibility, it can be disadvantageous to gaining employment as companies sometimes run the credit history of potential candidates, regardless of if it's a high or low paying job. Since there are no federal laws governing this, it is up to the states and their ever fluctuating laws that often provide little oversight.

Wrapping things up

Does everyone with a credit card end up with crippling debt? No. There are those who have the means, skills, and resources to manage debt but unfortunately this is not the majority of people. The fact of the matter is, debt isn't inherently good or bad (right or wrong), rather it comes with its own advantages and disadvantages. Some advantages include building credit, accruing points to fly, cash back, special perks for car rental or airport travel. The best benefit in leveraging debt is that you get to

Getting Into Debt

spread your risk. Meaning, if you are looking to finance a project and you borrow a portion of the seed money, if the venture fails, you are not left with 100% of the financial loss. Disadvantages include getting caught in a debt trap, lowering of your credit score, or paying excess fees. Keep in mind that there is a potential cost to utilizing financing options whether it be through fees, collateral that's put up, or your reputation.

Leveraging debt may be just what you need, or you may need to stay far away from it. Think about your relationship with money and whether or not it would allow you to play the debt game effectively. This has to be an individual decision and not one based on the fact that it worked for someone else. Remember, we all have financial situations as unique as our fingerprint.

Although I have participated in the credit market in the past to increase my credit score, that no longer is the case (for now) and I choose to purchase things with my debit card or cash. If I don't have the money for something in my budget, I don't buy it until I can afford it. My last big purchase took me 26 months to save up for. This lines up with my values because I don't like buying things I can't afford, and I don't like paying interest. This approach has its advantages and disadvantages and will not work for everyone. One drawback to this is if I decide to leverage debt (again) in the future, it could be somewhat challenging to get a line of credit in case of an emergency. To counteract this, I make sure to have multiple safety nets in place. I offer this as an alternative to the dominant belief that you must leverage debt in order to be successful in the U.S. when it's simply not the case. Educating yourself, making sound decisions based on your values and lifestyle, and your relationship with money are what will determine your long-term success and not whether or not you choose to leverage debt.

Key Takeaways:

- Debt is a big part of the American economy, but if you don't know the rules of the game you will get played

- Know your relationship status with money before you decide to leverage debt

Getting Into Debt

- There are several ways to increase your credit score, with credit cards and auto loans being the most common
- Before purchasing a house with a mortgage, do your due diligence
- Leveraging debt is neither good nor bad. How it's leveraged and how it's managed by *you* are the most important factors
- You can choose to buy everything in cash and avoid debt. This too has its advantages and disadvantages

Investing

Depending on your ultimate goals, there are many benefits to investing but overall, investing your money for the long term allows your future self to benefit from the work you are doing today. Ask yourself this question: do I have money from 2010? 2015? 2020? Or even 2 months ago? It is not enough to work every day and not have your future self-benefit from it. Investing allows your future self to benefit from today's work as the money grows from compound interest over time. Making money and then spending it all is a revolving door that doesn't allow you to get ahead. As you develop your saving muscles over time, you may be able to increase the amount you save if you decide to invest that money.

Before you start investing, make sure you have built up an emergency fund as mentioned in the previous chapters. Normally, I would recommend having 3-6 months of living expenses as emergency savings. What you would like to avoid is making investments just to have to liquidate those very investments 2-3

Investing

months later, because there is an emergency $500 car repair. That defeats the purpose of investing because profits more often come from investing in the long-term. Additionally, liquidating assets prematurely could result in tax consequences you may not have foreseen from inception. For example, a premature stock sale may lead to loss or any short-term gains you experience from selling stocks will increase your tax bracket i.e., the income which the IRS uses to determine your taxes owed.

CHECK THIS OUT!

Quick Tip on Investing

It is important to note that depending on your immigration status, you may not have access to certain investment vehicles/brokers as some do have restrictions. Nonetheless, there are more investment options available than not, so make sure you look at the requirements carefully.

It is also important that prior to investing, you start with a plan. Think of a financial plan as a roadmap: a map that gives you insight on

Investing

where you've been, where you are, and where you are headed, and how to do it. By starting with a plan, it will be easier for you to strategize which accounts/ investments may be right for your situation. For example, opening a retirement account is a good idea if you want to start saving today for wealth that you will use in retirement. Once you put your "retirement hat" on to strategize, it will be easier to distinguish which account has which tax implication.

Let's say you are 30 years old, and you start with a plan to be well off in retirement. That means you must start saving today in an account that will benefit you in the future, which would be at age 65 for this example. As mentioned earlier in the book, there are different types of retirement accounts. There are pre-tax Traditional IRAs and post-tax Roth IRAs. To oversimplify, with Traditional IRAs you pay taxes at retirement and with Roth IRAs you pay taxes now. Considering that you are 35 years from retirement, it would make sense to consider putting money in a Roth IRA so you are taxed today, and the funds can grow tax free for the next 35 years.

Investing

This is a simple example to illustrate how a financial plan can be of aid. By having a plan, you can let that dictate which course of action to take. Once you decide to embark on a specific course of action, then it will be easier to learn about the pros and cons to those specific actions. This strategy is better than learning about a variety of accounts/ tax implications that may not even be applicable to your specific situation.

You may also choose to invest in a non-retirement account. This means you have an investment account that is not restricted for retirement use; therefore you will not receive favorable tax treatment. This is attractive for those who want to yield higher returns than what is offered in deposit accounts and may want access to the funds sooner than waiting until age 65. As you start investing, it is important to note the different tax implications that may arise. You may be subject to capital gains if you make a profit on your investment. Alternatively, you may also be able to write off certain losses in your investments (depending on which asset was disposed of and for how long it was held).

Investing

When you sell a stock will also impact your tax rate, depending on if you kept that stock for more or less than a year. Typically, capital gains taxes are lower for stocks sold a year or more after they were purchased. With that said, these are not absolute, and things are subject to change, so it's always a good idea to consult an Accountant/CPA if you want a full evaluation of your financial liabilities.

As I mentioned in a previous chapter, if you are an immigrant, especially if your status is somewhat "uncertain", you want to do everything to reduce risk. One of the ways of doing so is to make sure all of your tax documents from your brokerage investment firms are disclosed at tax filing time.

Additionally, financial topics, especially investing, can be overwhelming and proper guidance is advised. This is not an endorsement, however, companies such as Charles Schwab and Fidelity offer financial workshops for the public, and clients also have the opportunity to discuss their financial health with a financial consultant. You can open an account for free at these firms and

Investing

> look to speak to a consultant, who would be able to give you 'tailor-made' advice, based on your specific situation. There are also local and state agencies or nonprofits that assist in personal financial management.

I always say that one of the most important things when it comes to investing is to start simple (no surprise here). The goal when investing your money is that $1 will increase in value over time and become $3. There is no right way or wrong way of investing, rather your investment type is heavily dependent on your overall goals and unique financial circumstances. With that said, the golden principle to investing is that the riskier an investment is the higher the possibility for a greater return/reward on your investment. The lower the risk means there tends to be a lower rate of return.

The reason most investments are structured this way is because there needs to be an incentive for investors to put their money in riskier endeavors (because uncertainty = risk). If this incentive of a higher pay out didn't exist, then start ups and other risky types of investments would not be as attractive. How you decide to invest will ultimately depend on factors such as your risk tolerance, timeline, values, and most of all your goals. As I stated in the beginning of the book, the objective is to touch lightly on these different topics so I won't discuss every single investment type, rather I will discuss the most common ones. Additionally, discussing the investment approach is more valuable for the purposes of this book than focusing on the specific investment types.

To touch on a few, you can invest your money in many ways, such as stocks, buying real estate, buying commodities such as gold, paintings, jewelry, or even crypto currency such as Bitcoin. Many people choose these different options based on their goals, but the principle remains the same—they are either trying to grow their money or preserve capital by investing their money.

Key points to consider when investing

1) GOAL: Having your end goal in mind is usually the best place to start as it will serve as guidance for which investment type is best for you. Once a plan is formulated, let the plan dictate which course of actions to embark on next. For example, are you looking to build wealth in general? Preserve capital? Fund your retirement or just save up for a vacation? Depending on what your goal is, there are different types of investments that may work better than others. After you have this figured out, think about what your values are.

2) VALUES: Your values are important to consider when it comes to investing as it can help create boundaries on what investments you are willing to do or not willing to do. For example, if for religious reasons you are against being involved with interest and the use of it, you may avoid investments such as money markets because they use interest. If you don't like companies that pollute the earth and that is part of your value system, this can also impact how you choose to invest your money. The point is that your values are important and if your investments are in line with your values then you are more likely to stick to them and make a profit.

As mentioned, long-term investing is how most people achieve success, so sticking to it is important. That's the case at least for me. One of my values is that I invest for the long-term, so I don't worry about the day to day market volatility. Meaning, if I put my money in an investment, it will be for the next 10+ years because I believe in long-term growth.

3) RISK TOLERANCE: Consider your level of risk tolerance: how comfortable are you with potentially losing money in order to get a higher return? Depending on your investment type, it may have higher or lower risk and return. Are you someone who may have a heart attack if you invest $1k and see $500 lost in a matter of hours? Are you someone who can leave money invested for long periods of time? Ultimately, your risk tolerance will be based on your goal for that money invested, your relationship with money, and your overall comfort level.

According to one of the Securities and Exchange Commission's website investor.gov,

> "An aggressive investor, or one with a high risk tolerance, is willing to risk losing money to get potentially better results. A conservative investor, or one with a low risk tolerance, favors

Investing

investments with low volatility. Many investment websites offer free online questionnaires to help you assess your risk tolerance. While the suggested asset allocations may be a useful starting point, it is important to have a review of your own account to make sure that the allocation of your actual assets match those of the model proposed."

4) TIMELINE: The timeline for your investment consists of how long you plan to keep your money invested and then liquidated. Is it a year? Five years? Thirty years? Will you pass on your investments to future generations and never liquidate? Timelines also play a big role in deciding where to invest. Investing for retirement compared to investing for your children or even wealth building, may have different implications on the amount of time your money is invested. Some investment vehicles are more advantageous for shorter, medium, or longer timelines.

For example, if your goal is to grow wealth and you won't need the money for at least the next 15-30 years, then typically a higher mix of riskier investments may be the way to go. This is because with that amount of time, volatility can be managed, and your investments are more likely to withstand the fluctuating value in your portfolio. As time gets closer to when you do need the money, it's common practice to allocate your investments into safer assets to avoid too much volatility and to preserve your capital. On the other hand, if your timeline is not 10 years but is instead 1 year or less, then it may be more advantageous to keep that money in a high-yield savings account or a money market fund to preserve capital. Though, this still will not give you full protection from inflation, it could potentially lessen the volatility of your capital, depending on the yield for the investment. Which just means you won't lose as much value in your money over time.

By investing in a cash equivalent account such as a high-yield savings account or a money market fund, it lowers your overall risk exposure, so you are less likely to lose value when the money is pulled out a year later. Is this rule full proof? Absolutely not. Nothing in finance is. The fact of the matter is, there is a small chance that you can be successful investing in stocks for less than 1 year and make a lot of money. But that would require you to be extremely talented or extremely lucky. The goal in investing for the long-term is to benefit from the gradual increase in stock valuations over a span of 10-20 years, which would consequently reduce the likelihood of loss due to short term stock fluctuations. Remember, risk can never be 100% removed.

CHECK THIS OUT!

QUICK CASE STUDY

Imagine you currently have $15,000 in cash with a goal of putting $25,000 as down payment for a house in five years. With this goal in mind, it may not make sense to invest all of your money in something extremely risky such as Bitcoin because you may lose value, especially considering a house is very important and it took a long time to save up that money. A common approach to this scenario is to invest that $15,000 into a low risk investment/savings account that you would be able to liquidate in a timely fashion, such as a high yield savings account, money

> market, bonds, etc. Short term goals such as purchasing this property should be about the preservation of capital and not growth.

How to start investing

In general, the most common way to successfully invest, but especially in the stock market, is to do so over a long period of time. Successful investing is long, boring and takes commitment. There are always exceptions to this, but this is what's most common.

1. First step is to have some type of plan or goal for the money you want to spend.

2. Then find a brokerage firm that works for you (Charles Schwab, Robinhood, Webull, Acorns, Fidelity, Chase are some of the most prominent ones). I recommend doing research by reading the company website information, watching reviews on YouTube from users of those accounts and getting general feedback from those you trust. Additionally, be sure to check if the

Investing

brokerage has any citizenship or permanent residency requirements.

3. Choose your investment. If figuring out which stock to buy is overwhelming, don't worry. It is common practice to not focus so much on individual stocks, but instead on index funds such as the Standard and Poor's 500 (S&P 500). Think of index funds as baskets that hold many stocks and if you invest in that one basket, you invest in all of the respective stocks it holds. There are other indexes besides the S&P 500, but I want to focus on the value of investing in an index which ensures that your money is diversified. Most people will not be able to directly purchase the index as it is expensive. The best way for the average investor to do it is by purchasing ETFs (that track the index) or mutual funds (that may replicate the index and try to beat it). There are many different types of investments to choose from, so make sure you do your research to decide what is right for you based on your goals.

Investing

One option that many people consider is using a financial advisor. This isn't absolutely necessary but there are many benefits to having one, especially if you have a considerable amount of money. If you are just starting out, it may still be nice to have a financial advisor as they can certainly help cut down on mistakes. But more than likely, if you follow the principles of diversifying your investments and sticking to them over time, you should be fine as well. Reading and educating yourself beyond this book is always encouraged as no one place can be your source for truth. View your financial journey as an ever continuing series of gaining information and making changes based on that information.

CHECK THIS OUT!

Key Investment Terms

Below are a few key terms to take into consideration when deciding to invest. Keep in mind that these are meant to be high level descriptions and do not contain all the details regarding these products. Please do more research on these respective investing instruments before deciding to utilize them.

- ❖ **Index funds:** Think of an index fund as a basket of goods that store many assets inside of it. Typically, in order to invest in a stock you would need to buy them individually. But index funds allow you to invest in multiple stocks (sometimes hundreds) at a time by just putting your money in one place. One of the most common indices is the Standard & Poor's 500 Index (S&P 500) which tracks the stocks of the 500 largest companies that are publicly traded

- ❖ **Mutual funds:** They are similar to index funds in the sense that you can invest in multiple stocks all at once. The difference is mutual funds are managed by a fund manager so there are higher fees involved. Additionally, there are restrictions on when you can trade. Mutual funds can only be traded at the end of the day and overall aim to beat the market in value creation.

Investing

- ❖ **Exchange-traded fund (ETF):** ETF is an index fund that you can trade all throughout the day unlike mutual funds. ETFs can be purchased on the exchange with any broker, whereas regular indices can be specific to a broker and are therefore not widely available. Overall, ETFs replicate the same stock investment as the specific index it's following but provides the flexibility of being able to buy and sell more freely.

- ❖ **Robo-advisors**: They make investing as simple and accessible as possible. You don't need any prior investing experience as robo-advisors create an investment strategy for you based on your goals and information provided. The benefit here is that it charges less fees to manage your portfolio compared to a portfolio managed by a human.

- ❖ **Stocks**: A stock is a type of investment that represents an ownership share in a company. Investors buy stocks that they think will go up in value over time.

❖ **Bonds**: Bonds—also known as fixed income instruments—are used by governments or companies to raise money by borrowing from investors such as yourself. Bonds are typically issued to raise funds for specific projects. In return, the bond issuer (governments or companies) promises to pay back the investment, with interest, over a certain period of time.

❖ **Certificate of Deposit (CD)**: A certificate of deposit is a time deposit, a financial product commonly sold by banks, thrift institutions, and credit unions. CDs differ from savings accounts in that the CD has a specific fixed term and usually a fixed interest rate.

❖ **Retirement accounts**: Simply put, retirement accounts are investment accounts used specifically for retirement. Below is a quick summary of the different types of accounts:

➤ Traditional Individual Retirement Account (IRA): Tax deductible contribution account that is taxed when taken out during retirement. This simply means you avoid paying taxes when you put the money in the account but instead pay taxes when you take the money out during retirement.

➤ Roth IRA: These are non-tax-deductible contributions, where withdrawals and investment gains are tax-free. This means you pay taxes on your retirement contributions as you invest but when pulled out during retirement you pay no taxes (the opposite of traditional IRA). This is a good option for long-term investors.

➤ 401k: This is very similar to an IRA. The big difference between the two is that employers offer

Investing

401(k)s, while you would open an IRA yourself through a broker or bank. IRAs typically offer more investment options; 401(k)s allow higher annual contributions.

➤ SEP: SEP IRAs are retirement accounts typically for self-employed people or small-business owners with few employees. Similar to traditional IRAs, the contributions are tax-deductible. Investments grow tax-deferred until retirement when distributions are taxed as income.

❖ **Options (not recommended for novice investors)**: Options trading is the trading of instruments that give you the right to buy or sell a specific security on a specific date at a specific price.

❖ **Crypto currency:** a digital currency in which transactions are verified and records maintained by a decentralized

> system using cryptography, rather than by a centralized authority.

CHECK THIS OUT!

Get Rich Quick!

Oftentimes, the Black community is more susceptible to receiving poor financial advice cloaked in the guise of 'getting rich quick' or 'getting rid of debt quickly' (which both are unlikely to happen quickly). These schemes are prominent on social media and come with a lot of risk of being coached or advised into poor decisions. These often include but are not limited to social media influencers parading as financial advisors or experts who target Black people. Social media 'real estate moguls' tend to lure Black people to invest in commercial real estate properties, advising them to start LLCs so they can apply for PPP loans and get cash quickly despite not actually having a business. These are real life examples of some

Investing

> of the schemes to look out for. Some may be genuine, but a lot are not.

Key Takeaways:

- Investing helps you to benefit tomorrow from today's work
- Before investing, have an emergency fund and a budget
- Before starting to invest, start with your end goal in mind
- Consider your risk tolerance and use it to guide you on your investment type choice
- Consider your values to make sure how you invest is in line with them
- Consider your desired timeline for investing as this will also impact the type of investments you go into
- Never stop learning and researching to improve your plan

Your Journey: Doing What's Best For You

Learning about your finances is no different from learning a new subject in school. If you were studying African history (actual African history), you could watch YouTube videos, read books and do your own research or, you can sit through a planned curriculum at Howard University with a professor that has a doctorate in African studies. While both approaches are valid and may help you succeed, studying at Howard University will most likely get you further and in a quicker manner than learning on your own. Similarly, when it comes to finances, continuing old habits and practices may eventually get you to a good place through trial and error (again, nothing wrong with this). However, learning from best practices and getting help from those with the experience (similar to studying at Howard) may yield better results. Regardless of the path you take, they all start with the decision to do something different than you have been doing, especially if it hasn't been working.

Your Journey: Doing What's Best For You

With all this information about your finances and so many options, how do you choose the right path for you? There is a lot of information, templates, suggestions, and videos, it can be difficult to know how and where to start. Don't panic. Based on your relationship with money, you will have your own personalized journey of discovering exactly how best to manage your finances. While there is no straight line for everyone, there are best practices and principles mentioned below that you can follow in order to save yourself time.

The first recommendation is to move past the discomfort of doing something different and make learning a consistent journey to absorb information that will eventually get you to where you need to be. This looks like listening to a 10 minute podcast every week on the different parts of budgeting or investing that you are curious about. It may look like doing a quick Google search on financial terms or having casual conversations with friends on why or why not to buy a house. It could also be reading short articles on the different aspects of personal finance. You can never learn enough about your finances because there is always a way to make your financial life easier and less stressful.

Many people leverage a fiduciary financial advisor such as a Certified Financial Planner (CFP), registered investment advisor (RIA) or fee-only advisor. According to a 2017 CNBC article by Kathleen Elkins, "A fiduciary has a legal duty to act in your best interest. Those not working to the fiduciary standard are held only to a suitability standard, meaning their advice must be suitable for your financial situation." There are financial advisors that specialize in specific financial tools and products such as life insurance, retirement, or investments. However, I recommend leveraging these professionals once you have decided that you need their specialized services because they may not be fiduciary. In trying to advise you, there is an inherent conflict of interest if their wage is commission-based and dependent on how many products they sell you. While it's not bad to leverage these professionals, I recommend going to them after extensive research or after speaking to a fiduciary advisor who will have your best interest at heart. Someone selling life insurance may advise you to get it because they will make a commission, even though life insurance may not be what's best for you. But once you are certain that you need their specialized service, they can be great resources.

I personally leverage a lot of the personal finance resources I have through my employer. If you do not have access to a free advisor, consider reading articles online and the many free resources on YouTube which I personally love. I will flag that not all information is good information, and it can be difficult to identify when someone is giving good genuine advice or if they are spitting BS. Be on the lookout for potential red flags. If someone giving you advice is closely linked with them selling you a product, that's a red flag. It's good practice to research the same topic from different sources so that way you can make connections on the consistencies and variations. When it comes to finance, there are an infinite amount of options and opinions and two people can give very different advice about the same topic and they *both* can be right. A lot of it boils down to your specific circumstances, which is why it's important to never take a one size fits all approach and to acknowledge your relationship with money.

Key Takeaways:

- Starting your financial journey can be overwhelming. Keep it simple and make it your own.

- There are advantages and disadvantages to taking formal or informal paths to learning. Just remember that there is no right or wrong path.

- Look out for bad information when learning about your personal finance. Learn to recognize the red flags and consider that there is no one size fits all in finance.

"Nah"... Setting Boundaries For Future You

"Yannick, can I have $500?" "Can you cosign on a house for me?" "I want to have a destination wedding and need to borrow $10K." Okay that last part didn't happen to me, but I have no doubt people have asked that before. How do you know when to say yes or no? And why is this relevant to your finances?

Setting strong boundaries is key to a healthy relationship with others, but most importantly, with your finances. A tip from Align Financial: "If you're setting boundaries for yourself, try sharing your personal journey with your loved ones. You know that best friend who encourages you to seize the day? You can tell her you're trying to eat out less to save money, but that you'd love to have her over for lunch at your place. If she continues to push you to spend money or eat out more, you may have to get more direct."

Without strong boundaries, many people find themselves out of money and resentful of the people they were trying to "save" financially. To start, setting boundaries has a lot to do with your sense of worthiness and whether or not you believe you deserve to put yourself first. For the most part, it's not as simple as saying no to everything. Being comfortable with disappointing others is a skill you need to practice so as to not compromise yourself because *you are worth it.*

CHECK THIS OUT!

Steps When Setting Boundaries:

- **Know your values and what you stand for**: At any given time, you can be faced with several decisions and many of them are financial. Values can help drive the decisions you make. Some people value family, some value going out with friends while others value building wealth. There is no right or wrong value, but each person will make different financial decisions in scenarios that they face based on what values they hold. The more you understand your values and what's important to you, the better decisions you will make because they will align with what's most important to you.

- **Have a budget**: In addition to knowing your values, leveraging your budget can be a very practical way of setting boundaries and making the right financial decisions. Whether someone asks you for money or you have the urge to purchase an item, taking a look at your budget to see if that is something that was planned for can easily help you decide whether to say yes or no.

- **Be comfortable and confident in disappointing others because you're worth it:** If and when you decide to set financial boundaries with others, it is likely to lead to negative emotions such as disappointment, sadness, or anger. That is okay. People are allowed to have their emotions, but the world does not revolve around those emotions. Practice being comfortable with disappointing others

> because the other option is to disappoint yourself. You should not make financial decisions that benefit others but would leave you in tremendous financial hardship.
>
> - **Be consistent**: Adults, just like children, will test your boundaries and it is up to you to reinforce those boundaries. It is not enough to say no the first time then say yes the third time, because you are teaching the other person that *your no is negotiable*. You have to maintain your boundaries the first time and the 10th time.

In a sense, my journey with boundaries has a unique flavor because I consistently contribute a portion of my salary to the family for different reasons such as school and making sure we meet our budgets. As a result, I want to give as much as I can while having enough for myself to meet my goals and pay for my monthly consumption of *Lamb Dibi and Suya*. This can become tricky because there is always a fine line between providing for others and not having anything left for yourself.

I got to a point where I realized I needed a plan to make sure my family was okay in the long-term and most importantly that I would also be okay. Consequently, being a bit selfish is actually healthy. A lot of people think that by being a martyr, sacrificing themselves, their needs and their wants all the time to take care of others, is the most caring thing to do. Being a martyr is not caring, rather it is you telling everyone else that you are not worthy of the very thing which you are giving. The article by Align Financial said it best: "Taking care of yourself is just another way of supporting your ability to take care of your loved ones."

> **Violation of your own boundaries does not entitle you to violate the boundaries of others.**

Oftentimes as immigrants, moving to another country can come with hardship and trauma. This could be from escaping a dangerous situation back home or from having to leave

"Nah"... Setting Boundaries For Future You

your family in order to live in another country and not to mention potentially living in poverty once you get to the U.S.

In any case, migrating and becoming the one who "made it" or is "successful" is a burden many people carry and without the right boundaries and understanding of this burden, it can lead many to make poor financial decisions that put themselves in a terrible situation. Some believe that giving everything they have, shows love, but what it actually shows is dysfunction. Oftentimes, people who violate their own boundaries may expect that others will do the same for them in the future. Naturally, this leads to resentment when others don't violate their own boundaries but instead maintain a healthy one.

For example, if a loved one asked you for $100 and lending that money would cause you to be late on your rent payment, it may not be a good idea. Let's say you lend the money and now suffer the consequences. When you ask them to cosign on a loan, but they say no, you may find yourself resentful because you violated your own boundaries but they did not violate theirs for you. Violation of your own boundaries does not entitle you to violate the boundaries of others.

> **A balanced approach is the best approach.**

As mentioned, there is a fine line between providing for others and being a martyr. I am not saying don't provide for your family or that you should always say no to friends. What I am saying is that usually a balanced approach is the best approach. You can't give something you don't have, so don't get to a point where all you are doing is giving and never having anything left for yourself. If so, you will get to a point where the very people who depend on you can't do that anymore because you haven't taken care of yourself and have nothing left to give.

One thing that helps me set boundaries is my **budget**. Because I have a planned monthly budget, whenever I'm asked for money or have unexpected expenses, I can go into my sheet and adjust as needed. If I'm asked for $100, my budget will say yes or no depending on if I allocated any money for donations or the particular expense in discussion. I may say no to

"Nah"... Setting Boundaries For Future You

the $100 but offer $50 because I know I can afford that. Depending on my relationship with the person who asks and the reason for the ask, I may say yes or no with the help of my budget. If I *trust* the person, there is a *good reason* for the ask and I can *afford* it, then the answer should be yes. But if any of those three things don't align then the answer is no. Most things in life are not straightforward because every situation someone asks for money is different. Know going into it that you will make mistakes and sometimes you should have given more or less than you did. Also know that you will improve overtime and you should not expect perfection. Ultimately, your budget is a tool to help guide you on what your financial decisions and boundaries are. But it is still up to you to set strong boundaries and stick to them. Expect that people will test your boundaries, but as long as you are consistent, they gon' learn over time.

I'm a strong believer that balance is needed in everything that you do. I love sharing my money, resources, and knowledge with people, but I also don't do those things to the extent that it takes away from my well-being (anymore). Additionally, don't let the boundaries you set completely dictate your life decisions to a point where it doesn't make sense. Just because you didn't budget for an Uber ride doesn't mean you shouldn't spend the extra money to get home at 3 a.m. instead of walking because Uber would be the safer option. Another example would be refusing to spend $5 on a sandwich during a busy day because you didn't budget for it and instead work all day while hungry. Balance is key. Be reasonable with the boundaries you set for yourself and others. Boundaries are meant to serve as a protective barrier and should at times be flexible.

Key Takeaways:

- Setting boundaries is a crucial skill to master in order to have a healthy financial relationship with others and yourself

- Giving everything and not having enough for yourself is problematic and will hurt your relationships in the long run

- Violation of your own boundaries does not entitle you to violate the boundaries of others.

"Nah"... Setting Boundaries For Future You

- Balance is key when trying to manage boundaries and you won't always get it right. But keep trying.

Money Shouldn't Be Taboo

In many Black/African cultures, talking about money is extremely taboo and can be one of the biggest cultural obstacles one overcomes when living in the United States. Regardless of how arduous or awkward it may be to discuss money, the consequences of not discussing it can be a lot worse in the long run. A 2018 CNBC article by Emmie Martin states that, "At the end of the day, it's important to understand that feeling anxious about money is normal, but it's also treatable. Financial anxiety is just a part of life now, but we do know that when we have a good comprehensive financial plan, we can reduce that anxiety and bring that peace of mind."

Not discussing finances with people you trust and/or live with can lead to misunderstandings and miscommunication about where everyone stands financially. There are many ways to go about solving this and a lot of it depends on who you live with and/or your family dynamics. Let's take a traditional family as an example where there is a mom, dad, and children. One way for them to manage talking about money is through monthly family budget meetings. Family budget meetings are an opportunity to bring stakeholders in a home together—they may or may not contribute to the finances. In these meetings, you will have the opportunity to organize your finances *as a collective unit*. This cooperative approach allows for far greater impact in all things you are trying to accomplish as a family unit and most importantly, transparency. This process allows you to look at your expenses, your collective income and plan for future expenses/allocation of funds.

While these meetings can have many benefits, they can also be very daunting given each person may have a different opinion on how much to contribute or where to spend money. There may also be power dynamics that adversely impact the decision-making process as the ones who make most or all of the money can at times have an unspoken power that others don't. In order for the family meetings to be successful, it is important that the group agrees on certain rules they will follow.

With so many voices, especially in large families, it is good practice to let everyone have a chance to speak regardless of who they are. Ideally, everyone should have input as to how the family spends the money because they are a member of said group or family, though elders and children may have different levels of input and decision making powers. Remember, just because someone doesn't work for wages, like a stay at home parent or child, doesn't mean that their work isn't an important contribution to the family. Every family is different but ideally, if a family has a retired grandmother, a student in high school, a full-time working parent and a stay at home parent, they can all have a say in how the family spends its money. This structure won't work for everyone but can be used as a model to build something that works for your unique scenario.

According to the CNBC article by Emmie Martin, a study found that "41 percent of Americans say financial stress impacts their relationship with their spouse and 45 percent say it leads them to miss out on social events. More than a quarter of respondents also reported feeling depressed on a monthly basis because of their financial situation." At the center of any healthy relationship is having good communication. As mentioned, communication goes a long way with establishing a financial life that works for everyone involved and will consequently relieve stress.

Let's say you are not part of a traditional household and you may live with roommates or by yourself, the same principles still apply as it is important to be able to communicate your financial situation in a manner that you are comfortable with. Whether it be conversations about paying rent, eating out or having a night out, it's important that you are able to communicate your boundaries around spending your money. Ultimately, you have a budget as well as other financial tools to help you achieve your goals and not talking about such things can make it difficult for others to understand or even support you in your very long journey. Furthermore, you will need support as there are so many moving parts, especially if you share finances or expenses with other people.

For example, if you budget $100 for groceries and you are living with someone who doesn't understand that concept or respect the importance of your budget, then they may push you to overspend your budget when you go grocery shopping for the house. That is when you might find it challenging to move forward or even find support in this relationship. You have to decide whether or not it makes sense to discuss your finances with this person and how much detail to go into so trust is important. This is also where boundaries come up and you will need to be consistent with them. Furthermore, you bringing up money could be a triggering point for some, especially with traditional conservative parents, partners or friends.

One of the most beautiful things I value about being Senegalese is that we are community oriented, and this is the culture in other predominantly Black countries. As a result, sometimes the mind frame is that "what is mine is yours." On the other hand, in the U.S. there is this myth that everyone is independent and should do things on their own. The truth is, no one is independent, and we all need each other. When you shop at the grocery store, you did not pick your fruit from a tree, nor did you ship it there. When you buy jeans, you didn't make it nor did you design it, other people did. Those who may be triggered by your budget or you talking about money are more likely triggered by the fact that you are challenging their notion of community (aka "what's mine is yours") or other cultural reasons, such as shared wealth and the values they grew up in. I would challenge you to embrace this value, while at the same time discussing money with boundaries. You can be family oriented while at the same time saying no. Keep this important value in mind when managing your finances, but also figure out what your boundaries look like so you can communicate them to others.

Key Takeaways:

- Talking about money with the right people is crucial to long-term success as you need external support from those around you

- Having structured cooperative discussions with family/friends/roommates can be powerful in organizing your money and getting the most utility from every dollar

- Discussing money can be taboo, so consider what cultural factors are at play beforehand

Understanding Amerikkka

A big reason I am writing this book is because as an African immigrant, I have had a very unique experience living in the United States. As such, I will outline some of the important lessons learned while navigating the different systems within this country. Keeping in mind that systems change and take on different nuances based on the cities and counties being referenced, for the most part I will discuss the overall system throughout the U.S.

As a Black immigrant, you may be new to the country or even a second generation immigrant, and as a result, you start at a disadvantage compared to the average U.S. citizen, because you do not have the benefits that come with several generations of knowledge, resources, and building of wealth. According to Pew Research, "Although Black immigrants have similar levels of educational attainment as Americans overall, their household incomes are lower than the median U.S. household. The median annual household income for foreign-born blacks in 2013 was $43,800. That's roughly

$8,000 less than the $52,000 median for American households." Someone who is part of a family that came to the U.S. from Europe in the 1900's has not only had the time to get used to the landscape, the language, and network of resources, but they have had a hand in weaving the very fabric of the socioeconomic policies in which we live under. You, as a fairly new immigrant, are at a disadvantage because you may not have access to certain information (or networks), and this results in inefficiencies and lack of opportunities. What tends to happen is you learn by making a lot of mistakes, which isn't an efficient process. This may apply to navigating higher education, filing taxes, or even getting a driver's license. One of the best ways to counteract this inefficient process is by tapping into a trusted network of people where you can get access to certain information or best practices.

If the typical U.S. citizen wants to start a business, they may ask family members for $20k, get a bank loan or go the venture capital route since numerous members of their family have owned their own businesses. This is one example of the advantages citizens may have that Black immigrants may not, because most likely they do not have a family member who can give them $20k. And if they go to a bank, they are more likely to be denied because of their skin color. But even if they are approved by the bank, they are more likely to be charged a higher interest rate because they are Black and especially if they have challenges with their credit score.

RACISM

Let's discuss racism: It is a set of laws, beliefs and practices systematically established as a way to disenfranchise Black people and other people of color, while artificially benefiting white people. As mentioned earlier in the book, regardless of if you consider yourself just Nigerian, Ethiopian, Jamaican or Senegalese, it is irrelevant to how you are perceived in the U.S. because you are seen as Black. This designation stems from the "one drop rule."

Black immigrants are the targets of racism and anti-Black policies before they reach the American shores with the legacies of colonialism, capitalism, and imperialism often being the reason they leave their home countries for the US. In 2018, President Trump referred to Haiti and African nations as "shithole countries." While not spoken with the same language, American foreign policy and media coverage of Haiti and Africa echo Trump's sentiments regardless of which side of the political spectrum they are on.

CHECK THIS OUT!

One Drop, You're Black!

The Harvard Gazette states that, "In the United States, the 'one-drop rule'—also known as hypodescent—dates to a 1662 Virginia law on the treatment of mixed-race individuals. The legal notion of hypodescent has been upheld as recently as 1985, when a Louisiana court ruled that a woman with a Black great-great-great-great-grandmother could not identify herself as 'white' on her passport." This is why President Obama was considered as the first Black President even though he was of mixed race. So frankly speaking, the state does not care whether or not you consider yourself Black. If you fit the phenotype of a Black person, then you will be

Understanding Amerikkka

> treated with the full distinctions of the Black experience (barring class distinctions). I mention this because many Black immigrants make the mistake of thinking they can separate themselves from this. While some do, the majority may learn the hard way.

As mentioned, racism is systemic, i.e., it envelopes every part of our society. It is a part of the very fabric that the U.S. was built on. So, for Black immigrants, racism can be very difficult to escape, therefore, it will most likely impact their finances. The manifestations of racism are so ubiquitous and so compounding that it is hard to fathom. With this in mind, we can see how Black immigrants are impacted by racism with everything from education, access to healthcare, housing, banking, food, and Artificial Intelligence.

> **The creation of whiteness politicized skin color and it created a dynamic and a source of political power to build the country known as the United States.**

Some of the clearest examples of racism include:

First, voter ID laws, which are policies that base voter eligibility on unique factors known to not be prominent in the Black community, such as having a driver's license. "On August 11, [2013], North Carolina's governor signed a voter identification law seen by many as an attempt to suppress the votes of people of color. After a lawsuit filed by civil rights groups and the U.S. Department of Justice, the North Carolina law was struck down by a federal judge who said it targeted African Americans with almost surgical precision."

Second, social policies structured as such that police are sent to deal with drug addiction in Black neighborhoods by use of force and violence, but in contrast the opium epidemic—which impacted majority white citizens—was seen as a health issue and treated with the appropriate resources, such as therapists and clinics. That is racism.

Third, when white neighborhoods are intentionally designed to have grocery stores, gyms and long spans of trees and grass that help to reduce heat in the summer, increase air quality and provide better mental health; meanwhile, Black neighborhoods are neglected, have corner stores with processed food, dilapidated public spaces and no area dedicated for nature, which results in hotter temperatures. These circumstances are not by coincidence, rather they stem from decades of racist policies. These are just some of the challenges Black citizens face and most likely Black immigrants face them as well.

CHECK THIS OUT!

Moving The Voting Goal Post

Voter ID tactics are nothing new. This racist practice is in line with Jim Crow laws that required Black people to pass test questions in order to qualify for voting. Questions included naming all of the U.S. presidents or doing complex calculations at a time when Black people had many roadblocks to education, and some were not allowed to read in the first place. Other examples include poll tests in South Carolina where

> Black people had to be able to read segments of the state constitution then explain what it meant, but the same requirements were not in place for white citizens. Some southern election offices would even have a giant jar of gum or other items and tell Black people to guess how many were in the jar. Regardless of the test, Black people "failed" even when they provided the correct answers and or information.

I have come to understand how daunting it may be for many Americans (white and Black) to acknowledge that racism/white supremacy exists as it would shake the very foundation of their entire belief system. Because if the country was built on a lie, what else in their life is a lie? If whiteness is the foundation of their value and self-esteem as a human being, it would be a devastating realization to admit that white supremacy is a lie. I fundamentally believe that we are all part of the human family. However, the creation of whiteness (which has not always existed) politicized skin color and it created a dynamic and a source of political power to build the country known as the United States.

On a more personal note, I have often been accused or suspected of stealing (and that's never been true). Consequently, when I go shopping I always keep my receipt and make sure I carry accessories in an obvious manner when walking in so that the cameras see that I have walked in with these items. Always keep your receipt. I avoid running at night as this can be perceived as suspicious, especially to the police. The last thing I want to give them is a reason and an excuse. As such, one should be mindful about how being a dark skinned, tall young Black man affects how you may be perceived in the world because being in the wrong place at the wrong time has different consequences depending on your appearance. As expressed in a 2020 Contemporary Economic Policy article, Class distinction too does little to reduce the impact of racism and anti-Blackness experienced by middle-class Black people. Despite having higher incomes and professional status than the average Black American family, Black middle-class families are not insulated from the adversity faced by the less well-off members of their race (Darity, Addo, & Smith, 2020. https://onlinelibrary.wiley.com/doi/full/10.1111/coep.12476)

> **CHECK THIS OUT!**
>
> <u>**How Racism Shows Up:**</u>
>
> - Black women are more likely to suffer from healthcare complications because of racism in the medical field. According to the CDC, "Black women are three times more likely to die from a pregnancy-related cause than White women. Multiple factors contribute to these disparities, such as variation in quality healthcare, underlying chronic conditions, structural racism, and implicit bias."
>
> - Artificial Intelligence was not designed with Black skin in mind, resulting in higher levels of mistakes when it comes to interacting with Black people. According to a 2022 Washington Post Article,

"Researchers in recent years have documented multiple cases of biased artificial intelligence algorithms. That includes crime prediction algorithms unfairly targeting Black and Latino people for crimes they did not commit, as well as facial recognition systems having a hard time accurately identifying people of color."

- The 1921 Tulsa Race Massacre. Local whites in Tulsa, Oklahoma were envious of the economic progress that the Black population had made nicknamed, "Black Wallstreet". So, they dropped bombs on them killing hundreds of Black people and destroying their homes and businesses.

- Teachers of all colors are more likely to perceive Black boys as troublemakers leading to higher rates of discipline which has created a school to prison pipeline. A 2018 Washington Post article states, "children suspended from school are more likely to drop out of school and become involved in the juvenile justice system...Students with disabilities represented about 12 percent of public school students, but accounted for nearly 25 percent or more of students referred to law enforcement, arrested for a school-related incident or suspended from school."

- White appraisers devaluing the value of Black families' homes. A 2021 Bloomberg article reported that, "Black couple saw the appraisal of their home increase by $500,000 after they took down photos of themselves in the house and had a white friend pose on their behalf during the appraiser's visit."

- The 1935 FHA Underwriting Manual stated, "If a neighborhood is to retain stability it is necessary that properties shall continue to be occupied by the same social and racial classes". This is code for: keep white communities

> white. The FHA discouraged banks from making any loans at all in urban neighborhoods, i.e., deny loans in Black communities.
>
> - In 2012, CBS News reported that in the mid-1950s the Army used motorized blowers atop a low-income housing high-rise and at schools in predominantly black areas of St. Louis, to send a potentially dangerous compound in the air to test their chemical weapons at the height of the Cold War.

ACCENT DISCRIMINATION

According to a 1993 New York Times article titled, *When an Accent Becomes an Issue; Immigrants Turn to Speech Classes to Reduce Sting of Bias*,

> "Speech has always been a popular indicator of education and intelligence…it is cosmetic. It has nothing to do with your logic, fund of information or ability to problem-solve." Later in the article, "Aside from

the differences of comprehension that thick accents may create, immigrants say that their experiences often reflect an underlying bias against them. Another layer of discrimination that is not often discussed is that of immigrants who have thick accents, especially those of Black countries. This discrimination coupled with racism can compound and be a heavy burden. Not only are people with thick accents assumed to have less intelligence but they are excluded from day to day activities because of their otherness."

Think of the racism spectrum in terms of deductions: the further away you move from whiteness and western European proximity in terms of appearance and speech, the more deduction in points you may experience, which results in more discrimination. The amount of points you have can influence your probability for success, access to certain spaces, people and jobs. For example, if you are a light-skinned Black African man with a french accent you will experience discrimination, but not as much as your African sister who has beautiful dark skin, a thick accent and a name far from Karen. Her appearance and accent is further away from the white/European standards, so she will face more discrimination than the lighter skinned African man. What does this have to do with personal finance? Many times, it's about who has the most proximity to whiteness and who can relate best to those in power that will determine how many opportunities you will be able to access. This isn't an excuse for not achieving your goals, rather it's something to be aware of and navigate.

WHITE SUPREMACY

White supremacy is a lie. White supremacy is the belief that those of European descent are superior and responsible for every human progress made, therefore, all socio, political and economic power should be diverted to them as a result. However, in reality white people, Black people and all people have invented and contributed tremendously to human history, so that we could survive and thrive. White supremacy lies when it says that white people discovered and invented everything and without them there would have been no advances in humanity. This is what is taught, and this too is a lie. Why does this matter? You will find that this false and absurd arrogance manifests itself on a daily basis by how you are treated, and you have to understand that root cause. Many white people feel that they are better than Black people, because of white supremacy and ironically Black people have also internalized this belief, as a means of survival. Conformity to whiteness is a survival tactic as—just as in the past—not conforming could lead to serious economic hardship or even death. In a 1998 interview on the Charlie Rose show, Toni Morrison said, "What are you without racism? Are you still strong? Are you still smart? If you can only be tall because somebody is on their knees, then you have a serious problem. And my feeling is that white people have a very, very serious problem."

Now that we have an understanding of white supremacy, what does it mean for the everyday Black immigrant? Having been in this country for 20+ years, I have noticed that racism doesn't allow the best and most qualified candidates to get the right jobs simply because of the color of their skin. Since society is structured to artificially benefit white people, but white men especially, Black immigrants are at a disadvantage when it comes to competing for a job even if they are the most qualified candidate. If we lived in a just world, the most qualified candidates would be diverse, and organizations would yield better production; hence benefiting capitalism and rendering the need for diversity and inclusion initiatives useless. So, if you are a Black immigrant and you ever feel that the game is rigged against you, it is. Nonetheless, success is doable with the right approach.

I have gone to school and worked with very impressive white people whom I admire. But others have gotten to where they are by being catapulted by their whiteness—especially when I know so many people of color who are more qualified than them. There have been so many instances where the white people I engaged with treated me less than because I was a dark-skinned African man. Don't be surprised if this happens to you even with the most well-meaning white people. It is not something I take too personally because in order for the United States, founded on genocide of Native Americans and the theft and enslavement of

African people, to exist as it currently does, there absolutely *had* to be the belief that someone who looks like me is less intelligent, less qualified and less than human. Remember the truth, white people are as human as everyone else.

> **CHECK THIS OUT!**
>
> **<u>Affirmative Action</u>**
>
> Michael Higgenbottom in the New York Times wrote that, "affirmative action is characterized as an unfair preference rather than a justified remedy". White women have been the biggest beneficiaries of affirmative action, yet they overwhelmingly oppose using race as a factor in hiring. A 2019 Pew Research poll found overwhelming support for the concept of increased racial and ethnic diversity in the workplace but also found disagreement with the use of race based affirmative action to achieve that goal. Affirmative action increased the number of women in the workforce, but as the employers were white men, they were more inclined to hire white women over non-white minority

candidates. Affirmative action benefited white women the most because outside of government issued contracts for Black folks, private sector white males had the final hiring decision and they picked white women first to satisfy affirmative action mandates.

Key Takeaways:

- As a first generation immigrant, you are at a disadvantage compared to the average U.S. citizen. Leverage networks to gain knowledge and save you time from making mistakes

- Racism is ubiquitous and is part of the foundation of the United States. As a Black immigrant, you will experience this on different levels

- Your proximity to whiteness, which includes anything from your skin color, hair texture, to your accent, will impact how you are treated. The closer to whiteness you are, the more points you get but ultimately you are not protected from racism.

Understanding Amerikkka

- White supremacy is a lie. Many Black immigrants have internalized this lie and it impacts our self-esteem

Money and Disabilities

Managing day-to-day life for an able-bodied person is stressful enough especially when you consider the hundreds of decisions made daily that impact their finances. For someone with a physical or mental disability, the difficulty is compounded because the person with disabilities has more hurdles to jump through every day, of every week, year after year. When you consider factors such as location, race, place of birth, economic status, etc. it can make it that much harder to survive or even thrive as those factors impact their ability to access the resources they need.

It can be difficult for someone with disabilities to manage their day-to-day financial decisions because the disability itself may not allow that person to fully trade their labor for money. The type of disability can also impact which jobs they qualify for. If the person is unable to walk, the number of jobs available to them such as package delivery are out of reach for the most part. This is all in addition to difficulties accessing quality education, a higher cost of living due to health care expenses, personal services, accommodations at home, and transportation. Whether the disability is mental or physical and in some cases both, the different hurdles layered on top of each other create a compounding effect making it more difficult to live.

CHECK THIS OUT!

Common Jobs for People With Disabilities:

- Cashiers
- Laborers/freight/stock/material movers-hand
- Janitors and building cleaners
- Customer service representatives
- Cooks
- Retail salespersons
- Stock clerks/order fillers
- Waiters/waitresses

Resources

Many countries that Black immigrants come from may lack the infrastructure to provide people with disabilities the resources to take care of themselves. Fortunately, in many parts of the U.S., people with disabilities can find much-needed assistance with their education, jobs, health care and much more. The downside is that these resources are not ubiquitous throughout the country nor are they equally accessible.

CHECK THIS OUT!

Tools & Resources to Consider for People With Disabilities:

- "The ABLE account is a planning tool that offers individuals with disabilities a tax-free savings option that does not interfere with the individual's eligibility for government benefits, such as Supplemental Security Income (SSI) and Medicaid. ABLE accounts are for US citizens or permanent residents, and it allows them to use saved money for qualified expenses. ABLE accounts do not need to solely be contributed to by the owner. Someone else may contribute as much as $15,000 (annual exclusion gift for 2021) for the benefit of a loved one in an ABLE account. ABLE accounts are easier to set up and manage than SNTs. These accounts come with some disadvantages—primarily, limits on the amount of money you can contribute each year.

- Special needs trusts (SNTs) are well-established savings tools that also protect eligibility for public programs. In some instances, it may be beneficial to create both an SNT and ABLE account. State laws differ on how they administer these tools, but you should consider them as they can be a good way to prepare for the future if you are someone with disabilities. If you are undocumented, depending on the state you are most likely not eligible to receive the SSI and Medicaid benefits anyway. SNTs don't have any such monetary limits as ABLE accounts but can be expensive to set up and more complicated to manage.

- Both ABLE accounts and SNTs allow a person diagnosed with disabilities—or their relatives—to save money without affecting their eligibility for public benefits.

- The Social Security disability benefits (SSDI) program pays benefits to people living with disabilities and certain family members

- Supplemental Security Income is a need based assistance program for food and shelter. It is a type of insurance, where you pay premiums every month and if you ever become disabled you can get paid.

- https://www.nfcc.org/: National Foundation for Credit Counseling® (NFCC®) is the largest and longest-serving nonprofit financial counseling organization in the U.S., with the mission to help all Americans gain

> control over their finances. The majority of these services are provided at no or low cost to clients and are funded by local grants from private sources and foundations, and client fees and contributions. These services are open to everyone.

In the U.S., the elderly are more likely to be the ones with disabilities due to health issues and a lack of quality preventative healthcare services. This is especially impactful in the Black undocumented community as elderly Black immigrants do not qualify for Medicare, because they are not U.S. citizens. Their citizenship status also impacts their ability to access Medicaid. Medicaid beneficiaries generally must be residents of the state in which they are receiving it. They must also be either citizens of the United States or certain qualified non-citizens, such as lawful permanent residents.

CHECK THIS OUT!

More on Disability Services

Disability employment services vary among jurisdictions. The ability to access such programming is linked to homeownership/head of household status and city and/or state residency. For example, in order to be eligible for Department of Disability Services in Washington, DC, an applicant must provide the following:

- Proof of District residency (i.e., a current lease, current utility bill, or a statement from Social Security with the address. Cell/telephone bills are not acceptable proof of residency)

- Copy of the person's birth certificate or government issued I.D., such as a drivers or non-drivers I.D., a Supplemental Nutrition Assistance Program (SNAP) card etc.

> - Copy of proof of health insurance (D.C. Medicaid or private coverage), if applicable.
> - Documentation that verifies the diagnosis of an intellectual disability prior to the age of 18 occurred, this includes school records/transcripts, medical records, or social history, if available (Department on Disability Services, https://dds.dc.gov/)

An article from the Migration Policy Institute stated that, "In 2006, almost half of all undocumented immigrants were uninsured, a level that is about three times higher than for native-born citizens. Because so many immigrants lack insurance, they face serious barriers to medical care and pay more out-of-pocket when they receive care." This lack of insurance prevents Black immigrants from completing the needed physical/mental assessments and evaluation needed to confirm diagnosis to qualify for disability employment services.

Discrimination and Income

While managing life with disabilities can be difficult, managing finances can also be a challenge, especially when someone else has control over one's money which oftentimes is the case. As it relates to income, the state in which someone with disabilities lives will impact their ability to earn a fair wage as laws may differ state by state. A 2014 report by researchers at the American Institutes for Research (AIR), a nonprofit and nonpartisan organization, found that "an earnings gap exists between people with disabilities and people without, and that gap widens as education attainment increases. Researchers also found that, in the working-age population of the U.S., people with disabilities were paid nearly 37% less than people without, even after controlling for labor supply and certain demographic and labor market characteristics."

According to the study by AIR, "the greatest earnings inequalities occur among those with a master's degree or higher. In 2011, nearly 28% of non-institutionalized people with disabilities in the United States, 21–64 years of age, lived below the poverty line, compared with 12% of people without disabilities. Nearly 10% of working-age adults have a disability. Part of this wage gap partly stems from discrimination in the workplace. People with disabilities are paid less, promoted less, and are given lower performance evaluations."

With all the discrimination against people with disabilities, there have been policies created to combat it. According to a 2020 HR Dive Article by Ryan Golden, Sections 501 and 503 of the Rehabilitation Act of 1973, prohibits discrimination on the basis of disability in programs conducted by federal agencies. The law also requires that contracts with the United

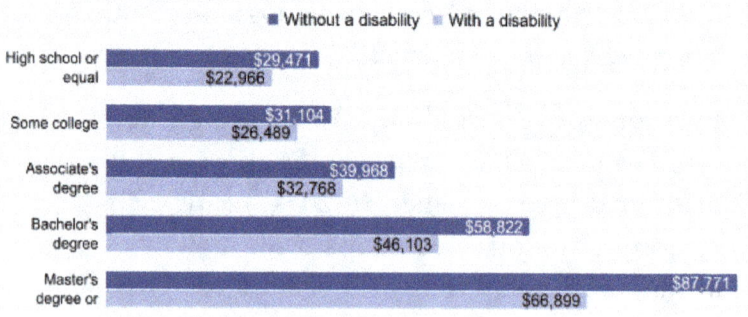

Earnings gap for people with disabilities widens as education attainment increases

Average 2011 earnings for U.S. workers by disability status and educational attainment

Ryan Golden/HR Dive, data from *American Institutes for Research analysis* of the 2011 U.S. Bureau of Labor Statistics American Community Survey

States make efforts to employ qualified individuals with disabilities.

People with disabilities are sometimes forced to stay at their place of employment because of the benefits offered, despite not being in a good work environment. This leaves them vulnerable and susceptible to abuse (similar to those with student loans who stay at jobs). Fortunately, nonprofits such as Disability: IN have created a network of resources for business disability inclusion worldwide. They work with over 400 corporations to expand opportunities for people with disabilities across enterprises.

Key Takeaways:

- Managing day to-day responsibilities is hard, with disabilities it's even harder
- There are many disability resources out there, but access to those resources is not equal
- People with disabilities face greater discrimination in the work place, which may lead to lower income
- Undocumented immigrants with disabilities have a greater challenge

Money and Disabilities

because they may lack access to quality preventative health care

Women and Money

"Since the start of the pandemic, more women than men have lost jobs, largely because so many women work in industries that have shrunk in 2020, such as the restaurant, retail, hotel and travel sectors." This is according to the American Association of University Women (AAUW), a nonprofit dedicated to advancing equity for women and girls. "The history of the gender and racial wage gaps is inextricably linked to the history of labor in America. From depriving Black women of wages while they toiled under the system of slavery, to creating lasting disparities in health, education, safety and opportunity, exploitation of and theft from women of color fueled America's economic growth, and those crimes continue to reverberate in women's lives today."

AAUW's study highlighted that, "After the abolition of slavery, policy makers and business owners prevented Black women from holding good-paying jobs…South Carolina's Black Code, for instance, prohibited freed people from practicing any trade without an expensive license, and then punished those who did not work by declaring them vagrants." Just as is the case with racism, gender discrimination operates in a systematic manner that holds back women from living and contributing to their fullest divine capabilities. According to the U.S. Census, on average, Black women were paid 63% of what non-Hispanic white men were paid in 2019. That means it takes the typical Black woman 19 months to be paid what the average white man takes home in 12 months.

The point of this chapter is to recognize this issue exists and that it affects everyone, especially when you consider that "80% of Black mothers are the sole, co-breadwinners or primary breadwinners for their households, a fair salary can mean the difference between struggling and sustainability for a family." The better off women are financially, the better society is because women are more likely to take care of children and lift them out of poverty. This idea is not new. Thomas Sankara, a pan-

Africanist, revolutionary and the first prime minister of Burkina Faso, was famous for recognizing the powerful role that women played and elevated Burkina Faso by promoting women. He put women in high positions of power, created economic opportunities and policies that protected their rights. Sankara once said,

> "The condition of women is therefore at the heart of the question of humanity itself, here, there, and everywhere."

CHECK THIS OUT!

The Pandemic and Women

- Between February and April 2020, women's unemployment rate rose by 12.8%, compared to 9.9% for men.

- Between the third quarters of 2019 to the third quarter of 2020, unemployment rose from 5.4% to 12.7% for Black women; 2.5% to 11.6% for Asian women; 4.8% to

> 12.5% for Latinas; and 3.7% to 8.6% for white women.
>
> - Mothers of young children have lost jobs at three times the rate of fathers. Moms of children under 12 lost nearly 2.2 million jobs between February and August, a 12% drop; fathers saw a 4% drop of about 870,000 jobs.
>
> - In the third week of July 2020, 32.1% of unemployed women ages 25 to 44 were not working outside the home due to childcare demands, compared to only 12.1% of men in the same group.

The AAUW study finds that:

> "Women with children face discrimination in the form of the 'motherhood penalty': employers are less likely to hire women with children (including those who never left the workforce), and they offer mothers lower salaries and fewer promotions than they offer to women without children. And because caregiving responsibilities still fall

disproportionately to mothers, women are more likely to take time out of the workforce, scale back their hours or postpone advancement opportunities. Meanwhile, fathers make 119% of what men without children earn."

A CNBC article by Megan DeMatteo highlights that, "Income disparity is a huge problem in the U.S. Even people working within the same industry, doing the same jobs make different salaries. Women on average make only $0.82 for every dollar a white man makes, but when broken down by race and disability, we see further disparities." The pay gap is a result of decades of discrimination in employment, intentional weak legal protections and pervasive racial stereotypes. When it comes to women, money, and labor, oftentimes the work that is acknowledged is the one tied to direct money payments. Generally speaking, work done by women is undervalued. In a traditional family, the father works, and the mother stays home to take care of the children. There is a power dynamic at play because the father is the one bringing in the money. But what is not usually acknowledged is the unpaid labor the mother does, often more than the father, which is absolutely needed for him to work in the first place. Another example is the mental load and logistical labor many women often hold when they have to figure out what the kids will eat, schedule doctor appointments, take care of loved ones' emotional needs, as well as keep the house clean, which all take energy and in the long run take a toll. This is not the case in every household but in many households, the overwhelming amount of labor (especially unseen labor) is done by the women. All of this unseen/unpaid work leaves women more financially vulnerable because it takes more time and energy to accomplish these things, and without the cash payment. This is compounded by societal expectations to get an education and a job. This vulnerability can sometimes lead to a lack of power and an inability to change living circumstances, which can be deadly especially when combined with poverty.

"Women are more likely to work in lower-paying jobs. In fact, they make up about two-thirds of the nation's low-wage workforce. Not only do these jobs pay poorly, but they are generally less stable and less likely to offer employee benefits, such as sick leave, health insurance and paid time off." During the 2020 pandemic, more women lost their jobs, had to double as teachers for virtual learning, and struggled with childcare more than men did. We tend to not assign value in these tasks that take a lot of energy, because money/payments are not directly tied to them and they have become unspoken expectations. But if those things went missing, we would definitely notice. The point here is not to say that men don't do anything, or to say that there is anything wrong with women doing these types of labor. Rather the point is to acknowledge that this dynamic is not by accident and by being aware of it, we can all work better to mitigate its adverse impact on women overall. It is not our fault that gender discrimination exists, but we are ultimately all responsible for creating a more just world.

Women and Money

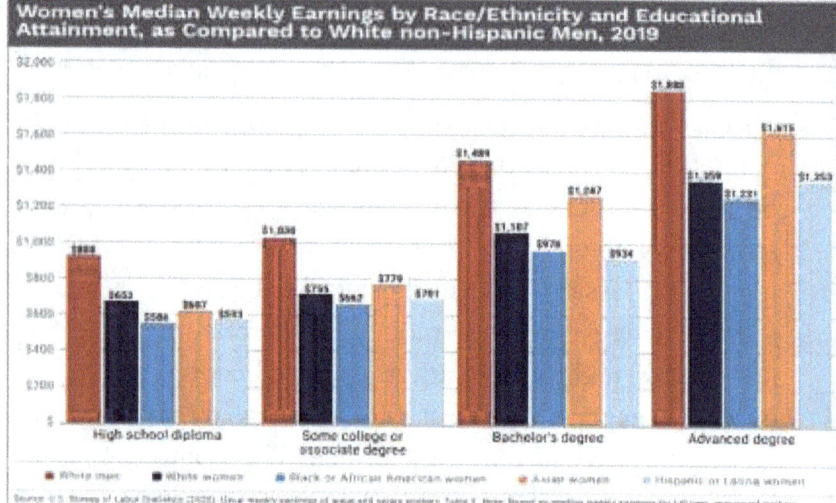

This graph demonstrates weekly earnings by demographics and the education level of women.

Women and Money

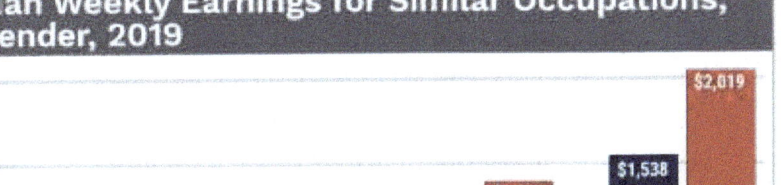

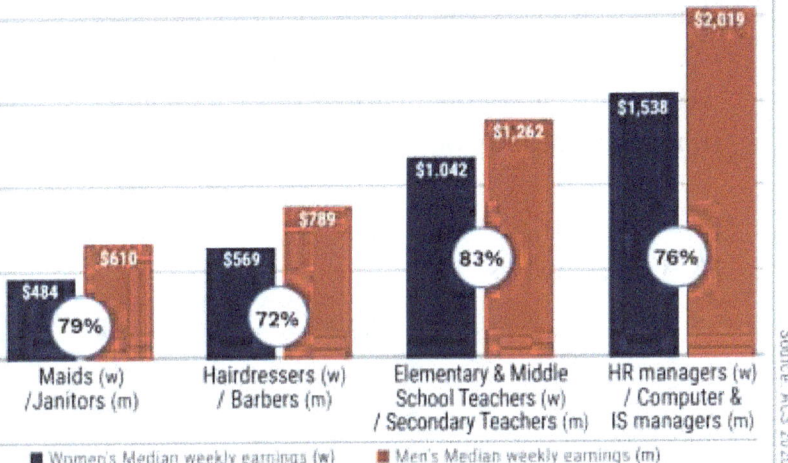

This chart demonstrates the pay gap between men and women by industry. On average, women make 80 cents for every dollar a man makes.

I have personally spent a long time reflecting on how I am either helping or hurting this issue. Growing up with three women (my mother and two sisters), I began to recognize how much work they do around the house and that it was not equitable. My brother and I, although we contribute a lot, did not grow up obligated to do the cooking or the majority of the cleaning. Cooking was mandatory for the women and an option for me and my brother. I started to show my appreciation in small ways by doing things like saying thank you, taking the lead on house chores/errands, and giving my sisters monthly stipends of a couple hundred dollars for their unpaid domestic labor of cooking and cleaning.

Key Takeaways:

- Just like racism, the gender discrimination holds women back from being able to achieve their full financial aspirations

- Women do a lot of invisible labor that is not tied directly to money, which leaves them more vulnerable to financial instability

- We all have a role to play in making sure we help and not hurt

CONCLUSION

The United States is a land of extremes; on one hand it is full of wealth and opportunity for growth, while on the other hand those very opportunities are afforded to a select few who know how to play the game. When it comes to managing your money as a Black immigrant, recognize the system overall was not created with you in mind, but you can still succeed. A big part of that success relies on your ability to understand and navigate the systemic guardrails that serve as obstacles. This simply means that you may be discriminated against at work because you are Black, you may not have the same educational opportunities as others because of your address, and you may not qualify for benefits because of your immigration status. Nonetheless, it's possible for you to succeed. This book provides guidelines for Black immigrants on structuring their personal finances with the context of living in the United States. Oftentimes, Black immigrants (like other immigrant groups) are not aware that there are rules to the game or of how the economic system is structured, therefore, time is wasted, money is lost and mistakes are made.

I have personally gained a lot of relief from writing this book. At the beginning of the COVID pandemic, I found myself relieved that my lifestyle had not changed after 6 months due to my planning and organizing of my financial life. Every day, I was reading about people who lost their jobs and all of a sudden found themselves on the street. Unlike during the 2008 recession, I was okay. I had my job but even if I didn't, I knew that I could live one year without having to change my lifestyle because I spent several years developing and executing a financial management plan. I also found myself reaching out to friends and vice versa to discuss how to set up a budget. I found myself passionate about the topic, but even more so, frustrated that I did not have a platform to provide all of the knowledge I had learned during my 21 years in the United States to many people all at once. Out of the blue came the desire to write a book. After much doubt, I realized that my voice was needed because it represents millions of people. I recognized in all of my research that most financial advice is geared towards upper class white men. There are not many financial resources that consider the nuances that many Black immigrants may face. From then, I spent 4 months drafting this book and then called my contributing editors to get involved. It took me three years to complete.

I hope with all that I have outlined, it has become clear that managing your finances has many layers and is heavily impacted by our current and historical context. Nonetheless, if done right, it can have a tremendous long-lasting positive impact on you and potentially those around you. Money has very little to do with how smart you are but rather how you behave. The average person with no financial background can be wealthy if they have a handful of behavioral skills. As a Black immigrant, you must be intentional about your financial management because you have more obstacles than the average person and you have more to lose. "Always remember, finances and money are not the goal, they are the tools to get you to the goal. So, figure out what the goals are and then figure out how to structure your finances accordingly." -DIY Money Podcast.

The Concept
Cover Art

The title of the book "Doundale" is a word derived from Wolof, the main language spoken in Senegal, which means to live and thrive. I was intentional in making sure the cover art was a visual representation of the intent for the book. My hope is that with the information presented, Black immigrants will be able to implement the financial tools and strategies in their lives to not only survive but also thrive.

The floral patterns are from the Baobab tree also known as "the tree of life" flowing in abundance all throughout the cover. It includes the leaves, flower and the fruit of the Baobab. Additionally, I have included currency to represent the financial focus of the book. Lastly, I was intentional about the color scheme of the cover; the distinct red, black, and green from the Honorable Marcus Garvey flag created in 1920 as a symbol of freedom, pride, and the political power of Black Americans.

Marcus Garvey

Marcus Garvey was a Jamaican-born Black nationalist and leader of the Pan-Africanism movement, which sought to unify and connect people of African descent worldwide. Marcus Garvey was regarded as one of the most notable civil rights leaders in the 1920's having founded the Negro World newspaper, a shipping company called Black Star Line and the Universal Negro Improvement Association, or UNIA, a fraternal organization of black nationalists. He influenced countless future leaders including Malcom X.

Baobab Tree

The Baobab tree is a symbol of the African spirit representing strength, dependability, and resilience to name a few. These characteristics are what allow generations of immigrants to travel thousands of miles away from their homeland to a place that is unfamiliar, with a different language, a different system all with the hopes of economic opportunity and prosperity.

The Baobab is known as the "tree of life" because of its versatility in how it benefits the day-to-day life of African people. Besides being such a striking landmark, a large tree has the capacity to store up to 4,500 liters of water, has fruit and leaves that are edible, and not to mention its important role in traditional practices and treatment of ailments. Its natural habitat is the extremely dry and arid climate of the African savannah; therefore, it is a symbol of life and positivity in a landscape where little else can flourish with little water.

Every part of the Baobab tree is valuable – the bark, can be made into rope, worn as clothing, and used to treat common ailments. The seeds can be used to make oils for cosmetics, the leaves can be eaten, and the fruit is exceptionally high in nutrients not to mention absolutely delicious! In addition to serving as a source of food, shelter, clothing, and medicine, the trees in West Africa have also been used as burial sites for oral tradition griots. One explanation for why they were buried in baobabs is because these men were living historians, walking libraries, and the words that they spoke held significant power, their energy should radiate throughout the baobab for all of eternity. As the tree is revered to a sacred tree that stands for wisdom and a long life, it was chosen as the final resting place for the griots. For this reason, it is taboo to cut down.

Baobabs have been known to live for over a thousand years, making them one of the oldest living things on the planet. Its hardiness and size have rendered it immune to most of the effects that the climate and environment have on it. They are notoriously difficult to kill and can even regrow their bark after being stripped of it or burned.

For these reasons, I have decided to make the Baobab the symbol for the book, and a representation of the strong resilience and perseverance demonstrated by Black immigrants every day. Despite facing economic hardship, discrimination, racism, and other challenges, we still get up to work and study so we can take care of our children, our family back home and most importantly ourselves.

Book Summary

Purpose: This book provides guidance for Black immigrants on structuring their personal finances with the context of living in the U.S. Oftentimes, Black immigrants (like other immigrant groups) are not aware that there are rules to the game, or know how the economic system is structured; therefore, time is wasted, money is lost, and mistakes are made. I focus on targeting Black immigrants because for so long, our needs have been ignored and our experiences not recognized. In this book, I discuss the basics of financial management, making financial decisions, and navigating the system in the U.S. to ultimately increase your chances of success, and have less financial stress in your life.

Background: One reason for me writing this book is because I want to share the relief that having a financial management system has brought me. Unfortunately, not all of us have equal access to these tools and information which can lead us to make poor financial decisions. If your finances run you instead of the other way around, it is your responsibility to make that change and this book will teach you how.

What's your Relationship $tatus with Money: Your past experience with money, good or bad, greatly impacts your current spending habits and your overall financial plan. Knowing your relationship status with money can help you in making strategic decisions about your finances and implement the most effective solutions. In the past, you needed money for almost everything you did. So it makes sense that these past experiences impact your view of money today.

Start with $5: The best way to start most things is often the simplest way. Planning out your financial picture can be daunting, overwhelming and bring up feelings of anxiety. The reason is that our past relationship with money impacts how we view and deal with money today. So much so that the very thought of creating a budget makes you nauseous. Starting simple is the answer: create 5 line items that are the most important to you and that you want to track. You don't need to have your full budget or all of it figured out at once. While this journey can be challenging, the consequences of not having a plan is so much worse than the discomfort of creating a plan. So, start slow, take your time, and listen to your emotions and most importantly: ask for help!

Issa WHOLE Budget: A budget is a plan of how you will spend your money. Having and using a budget is one of the best tools to help you in your financial journey. Many people don't use a budget because they may find it overwhelming or don't know how to incorporate it into their life. We'll discuss how to get started, the pitfalls, and how to fit it into your life.

Creating Your Safety Nets: As a first or second generation Black immigrant, you may be more vulnerable to economic distress because the social safety nets may not be accessible to you as much as for others. In general, there is a very thin social safety net in the U.S. as most expenses are carried on the individual level as opposed to the governmental level. When you are responsible for health care, housing, food and other major expenses, any major event or disruption can leave you financially distressed and you are more likely to suffer economically.

This is why it is important to build those social safety nets such as cash reserves, having the right insurance, having a network of people you trust and most importantly making smart financial decisions.

Getting Out of Debt: Regardless of your debt burden, you can get out of it…with the right plan. Having lingering debt sucks your liquidity each month and hinders you from creating margin, saving money and in some ways can even stop you from leaving a bad job. This chapter discusses different strategies in managing your debt and how to realistically get out of it.

Getting Into Debt: one consequence of not having safety nets is you may end up going into debt. Debt in itself is not a bad thing but having it may adversely impact your month to month liquidity and strain your ability to get ahead financially. Where people go wrong with managing debt is first and foremost not having the tools and skills to manage it. Consider this and your relationship with money before taking on debt, as well as make sure it is in line with your long-term financial goals

Investing: The value of investing is that you have your money working for you. But not everyone should dive into investing because there is risk involved and things to do before investing. Consider having an emergency fund before investing because if anything happens, you may need quick cash and won't be able to wait to liquidate stock, gold jewelry or even an investment property. Also, consider things like funding for your retirement and other goals. Investing is not for everyone and you should evaluate the value proposition on an individual basis. But for most people with an effective financial plan, investments are a great way to diversify your assets and let your money grow.

Your Journey: Doing What's Best For You: Take the time to make your financial plan your own. You cannot expect to have a perfect plan in the beginning. Expect some setbacks and bumps, because anything worth having taken time and patience to develop. As you learn new information, make slight changes that you think are appropriate. Set a plan and have the flexibility to make changes if need be. As with anything else, a balanced approach is usually the right one. Make slight tweaks along your journey until you reach your goals. And once you get there, set new ones.

Nah...Setting Boundaries For Future You: We have red lights for a reason, we have driving lanes for a reason, we even have doors that open and close. They all serve as visual cues for when to stop and when to go. The end and the beginning. Where it is okay and not okay to step on to. The difference between those boundaries and human boundaries is a question of visibility. Boundaries are part of a strong foundation in any relationship and you cannot have a healthy financial plan without knowing what your boundaries are, and most importantly, how to enforce them. Enforcing boundaries is how humans essentially make them visible and easy for others to follow—similar to red lights and driving lanes. Making $1 million doesn't mean anything if you don't have boundaries to manage it and you end up just giving it away.

Understanding Amerikkka: Even with all of your might and will to succeed, know that there will come times when things are simply out of your control and because of the color of your skin, gender or sexual orientation, you will be discriminated against. This is part of the very fabric of the United States' socio, political and economic system. The U.S. is founded and run on white supremacy and unfortunately, this permeates everything. This is not to say that you cannot succeed and achieve your goals. It is to say that despite white supremacy, you can still achieve your financial goal.

Money Shouldn't Be Taboo: Depending on your culture, country or family, discussing money can be taboo. It can often bring up feelings of shame, inadequacy, guilt, anger. Or it can bring up excitement, joy, hope and exuberance. Money by itself doesn't actually hold value, rather we as humans assign value to it. Similarly, money by itself does not hold any specific emotions, we as humans assign emotions to it. Our emotions about money are mainly influenced by our past relationship with money. Having insight into your past and emotions are huge steps in removing barriers and obstacles that are preventing you from having the financial plan that you dream of.

Money and Disabilities: It is very challenging to manage your personal finance as someone with disabilities. The disabled make less income on average but also tend to have higher healthcare costs which make it difficult to manage their lives. If qualified, it is important for those that are disabled to seek out resources and tools such as ABLE accounts that can assist them.

Women and Money: It is important to realize that there is a particular dynamic women deal with regarding money that impacts them differently than men. This dynamic can be perpetuated by men and women. Sexism is the invisible and visible hand that works to shift political, social, and economic power away from women, under the belief that they are inherently inferior. From a financial perspective, it is important especially for women to create their own respective safety nets as women tend to be more vulnerable in marriage, they spend more time doing domestic work at home and even carry more emotional burden–all things that don't result in direct income.

References

'One-drop rule' persists – Harvard Gazette. https://news.harvard.edu/gazette/story/2010/12/one-drop-rule-persists/

"United States : HUD Announces $630,000 Agreement with Illinois Property Owners, Managers Accused of Discriminating against Applicants with Disabilities." MENA Report, Albawaba

(London) Ltd., May 2016, p. n/a.

4 Ways to Determine Your Debt Tolerance - cnbc.com. https://www.cnbc.com/select/how-to-determine-debt-tolerance/

5 Reasons Why Personal Finance is More Complicated Than You Think - CNBC. https://www.cnbc.com/select/why-personal-finance-is-complicated/

An Uneven Playing Field: The Lack of Equal Pay for People with ... - AIR.
https://www.air.org/sites/default/files/Lack%20of%20Equal%20Pay%20for%20People%20with%20Disabilities_Dec%2014.pdf

Assessing Your Risk Tolerance | Investor.gov.
https://www.investor.gov/introduction-investing/getting-started/assessing-your-risk-tolerance

Black Women and the Pay Gap: AAUW.
https://ww3.aauw.org/article/black-women-and-the-pay-gap/

Black Women Three Times More Likely to Die from Pregnancy-Related ....
https://www1.cbn.com/cbnnews/health/2022/april/black-women-three-times-more-likely-to-die-from-pregnancy-related-causes-than-whites

Considerations for Estate Planning for Immigrants | Blog | Jenkins ....
https://www.jenkinsfenstermaker.com/blog/estate-planning-for-immigrants/

Daily Journal. https://www.dailyjournal.com/articles/367588-women-s-wages-and-the-california-fair-pay-act

Eligibility for DC Services - Total Care Services, Inc.. https://totalcare1.org/what-we-do/dc-services/eligibility-for-dc-services/

Good debt vs. bad debt: Why what you've been told is probably wrong - CNBC. https://www.cnbc.com/2020/07/20/good-debt-vs-bad-debt-why-what-youve-been-told-is-probably-wrong.html

How To Determine Your Debt Tolerance | Advisorpedia.

https://www.advisorpedia.com/viewpoints/how-to-determine-your-debt-tolerance/

Implicit racial bias causes black boys to be disciplined at school more ....

https://www.washingtonpost.com/news/answer-sheet/wp/2018/04/05/implicit-racial-bias-causes-black-boys-to-be-disciplined-at-school-more-than-whites-federal-report-finds/

Money is more stressful than work or relationships - CNBC.
https://www.cnbc.com/2018/06/26/money-is-more-stressful-than-work-or-relationships.html

Robots trained on AI exhibited racist and sexist behavior - The....
https://www.washingtonpost.com/technology/2022/07/16/racist-robots-ai/

SIMPLE THE TRUTH - AAUW. https://www.aauw.org/app/uploads/2020/12/SimpleTruth_2.1.pdf

Statistical Portrait of the U.S. Black Immigrant Population | Pew https://www.pewresearch.org/social-trends/2015/04/09/chapter-1-statistical-portrait-of-the-u-s-black-immigrant-population/

SYSTEMIC RACISM AND THE GENDER PAY GAP - AAUW. https://www.aauw.org/app/uploads/2021/07/SimpleTruth_4.0-1.pdf

The Affordable Care Act & Mixed-Status Families. https://www.nilc.org/issues/health-care/aca_mixedstatusfams/

The Nature of Work and the Social Safety Net | Urban Institute.

https://www.urban.org/research/publication/nature-work-and-social-safety-net

The Racist History of Tipping - POLITICO Magazine.
https://www.politico.com/magazine/story/2019/07/17/william-barber-tipping-racist-past-227361/

The social safety net: The gaps that COVID-19 spotlights.
https://www.brookings.edu/blog/up-front/2020/06/23/the-social-safety-net-the-gaps-that-covid-19-spotlights/

Toni Morrison Interview on White Supremacy and Racism in 1993 ... - Esquire.
https://www.esquire.com/entertainment/books/a28621535/toni-morrison-white-supremacy-charlie-rose-interview-racism/

Understanding the Facts About Critical Race Theory - DemCast.

https://demcastusa.com/2021/06/23/critical-race-theory/

Voting Rights: A Short History - Carnegie Corporation of New York.

https://www.carnegie.org/our-work/article/voting-rights-timeline/

Welfare Lifts up White Middle Class, Largely Excludes Black Americans.
https://www.businessinsider.com/welfare-policy-created-white-wealth-largely-leaving-black-americans-behind-2020-8

What Are Money Boundaries and Why Are They Important?.
https://www.align.financial/what-are-money-boundaries-and-why-are-they-important/

What Happens If You Don't Use Your Credit Card? - Yahoo! News.

https://news.yahoo.com/happens-dont-credit-card-214050702.html

What It Will Take to Close the Race Gap in Home Appraisals.
https://www.inclusivityinstitute.org/news/what-it-will-take-to-close-the-race-gap-in-home-appraisals

Why do pay gaps persist for US workers with disabilities?.
https://www.hrdive.com/news/why-do-pay-gaps-persist-for-us-workers-with-disabilities/581533/

Why Equal Pay Matters | Illinois Fox Valley SHRM.
https://illinoisfoxvalley.shrm.org/events/2020/08/why-equal-pay-matters

Why health care costs are making consumers more afraid of ... - CNBC.
https://www.cnbc.com/2018/04/22/why-

health-care-costs-are-making-consumers-more-afraid-of-medical-bills-than-an-actual-illness.html

Why it's important to know what fiduciary means - CNBC.
https://www.cnbc.com/2017/09/13/why-its-important-to-know-what-fiduciary-means.html

Will a Credit Card with Zero Balance Hurt My Credit Score? - WalletHub.
https://wallethub.com/edu/cs/credit-cards-without-balance/25555

www.ingramcontent.com/pod-product-compliance
Lightning Source LLC
Chambersburg PA
CBHW070422010526
44118CB00014B/1865